*Conversational*

# FRENCH

# IN 7 DAYS

SHIRLEY BALDWIN & SARAH BOAS

**PASSPORT BOOKS**
a division of *NTC Publishing Group*
Lincolnwood, Illinois USA

# ACKNOWLEDGMENTS

The authors and publishers are grateful to the following for supplying photographs or illustrations:

Barnaby's Picture Library (cover, pp. 27, 48)
J. Allan Cash Ltd (p. 1)
Keith Gibson (pp. 16, 20, 21, 33, 34, 35, 39, 43, 44, 45, 47, 53, 59, 60, 61, 65, 68, 73)
The French Government Tourist Office (pp. 3, 22, 29, 61, 66)
RATP: Metro and RER maps (pp. 19, 21)

**Photo credits**

front cover:
*top & middle*  Keith Gibson
*bottom*  French Government Tourist Office

back cover: Keith Gibson

**1996 Printing**

This edition first published in 1991 by Passport Books,
a division of NTC Publishing Group,
4255 West Touhy Avenue, Lincolnwood (Chicago),
Illinois 60646-1975. Originally published by Hodder & Stoughton Publishers.
©Shirley Baldwin and Sarah Boas, 1988. All rights reserved.
No part of this book may be reproduced, stored in a retrieval system, or
tansmitted in any form, or by any means, electronic, mechanical, photocopying,
or otherwise, without the prior permission of NTC Publishing Group.
Manufactured in Hong Kong.

6 7 8 9 0 WKT 9 8 7

# CONTENTS

# INTRODUCTION

**Conversational French in 7 Days** is a short course that will equip you to deal with everyday situations when you visit France: shopping, eating out, asking for directions, changing money, using the phones, and so on.

The course is divided into 7 units, each corresponding to a day of the life of Patrick (a designer) and his cousin Claire during their week in France. Each unit begins with a dialogue, which introduces the essential language items in context. Key phrases are highlighted in the dialogues, and the phrasebook section that follows lists these and other useful phrases and tells you what they are in English.

Within the units there are also short information sections in English on the topics covered, sections giving basic grammatical explanations, and a number of follow-up activities designed to be useful as well as fun. Answers can be checked in a key at the back of the book. English-French vocabulary is listed under topic headings on pp. 80–83, followed by a French-English vocabulary list. Accompanying this book, 2 cassettes will help you practice your French.

## Pronunciation

*Do* stress the last syllable more than the others.
*Do* run two words together when one word ends in a consonant and the next starts with a vowel: **vous êtes, nous avons**.
*Don't* pronounce the consonant at the end of a word (except those ending in **c,f,l,r**).
*Don't* pronounce **e** at end of words (*except* in one-syllable words or when it is accented).

### Vowels

**a** as in *father:* valise [vahleez]
**a, â** as in *baa:* pas [paa]
**e** as in *sun:* je
**e, é, er, ez** as in *Spain;* et [ai]
**e, è, ê, ai** as in *pen:* père [pehr]
**e, eu, œ,** as in *over:* deux
**i** as in *feet:* valise
**o, ô, eau, au** as in *low:* hôtel
**o** as in *old:* votre [votr]
**u** as in *few:* une [ewn], numéro
**ou** as in *loot:* tout [too]

### Nasalized vowels

**am/an** like *taunt:* grand [grah(n)]
**em/en**       en [ah(n)]
**im/in**       fin [fa(n)]
**ain/ein**     pain [pa(n)]
**om/on**       bon [boh(n)]
**um/un** like *earnest:* lundi [luh(n)dee]

### Semi-vowels

**ui** like *sweet:* oui [wee]
**oi/oy** like *swan:* moi [mwa]
**ll** like *yet:* cuiller [kwee-yer]
**ail** like *pie:* travail [tra-vye]

### Consonants: similar to English but with the following exceptions:

**c** before *i* or *e* like *sun:* c'est
**ç** always like *sun:* ça
**ch** like *shun:* chant
**g** before *i* or *e* like *leisure:* voyage
**gn** like *union:* montagne

**h** always silent: l'hôtel [lotel]
**j** like *leisure:* je
**qu** like *can:* quarante
**r** tongue at back of mouth; merci

# SAYING HELLO AND GOODBYE

**Arrival**   When arriving at a port or airport, you will find customs and passport procedures standard and easy to follow, because most information is given in English as well as in French. You should check duty-free allowances before setting out on your trip. Look out for the sign DOUANE (*Customs*).

## l'arrivée/the arrival

Patrick and his cousin Claire are traveling to France together. They disembark at the hoverport.

"Mesdames et Messieurs, nous vous remercions d'avoir voyagé avec nous et espérons vous revoir bientôt à bord." (*Ladies and gentlemen, thank you for traveling with us. We hope to have you on board again soon.*)

| | |
|---|---|
| Hôtesse: | (to Patrick and Claire) **Au revoir et bon voyage, monsieur-madame**. |
| Patrick et Claire: | Au revoir, mademoiselle et merci. |

Patrick (22, director of a small design firm, is met by his French agent, Bernard Rousseau.

| Bernard: | **Bonjour, monsieur. Vous êtes** M. Vincent? |
| Patrick: | **Oui, je m'appelle** Patrick Vincent. |
| Bernard: | **Je me présente.** Je suis Bernard Rousseau. |
| Patrick: | **Ah, bonjour** Bernard. **Enchanté de faire votre connaissance.** |
| Bernard: | Donnez-moi votre valise, s'il vous plaît. La voiture est là-bas. L'hôtel est tout près. |
| Patrick: | Merci beaucoup. |

Clair (17) is met by the French family she is going to stay with.

| Mme Bergeron: | **C'est vous,** Claire Rogers? |
| Claire: | **Oui, c'est moi.** |
| Mme Bergeron: | **Je suis** Madame Bergeron, **et voici** mon fils, Julien. **Comment ça va?** Vous avez fait un bon voyage? |
| Claire: | Oui, très bien merci, madame. |
| Julien: | Dépêchons-nous, maman. Le taxi attend. |
| Mme Bergeron: | Eh bien, Julien, prends les bagages. |

▶▶ **Saying hello and goodbye**  In France, people generally shake hands each time they meet and when saying goodbye. Always address a man as **monsieur**, and a woman as **madame**, or **mademoiselle** for a young girl or if you know she is not married.

| | |
|---|---|
| **Bonjour, monsieur.** | Hello (to a man). |
| **Bonsoir, madame.** | Good evening (to a woman). |
| **Salut! Comment ça va?** | Hello! (to a friend) How are things? |
| **Ça va bien, merci.** | Fine, thanks. |
| **Comment allez-vous?** | How are you? |
| **Très bien, merci.** | Very well, thank you. |

### Introducing yourself

| | |
|---|---|
| **Je m'appelle . . .** | My name is . . . |
| **Je me présente . . . Je suis . . .** | Let me introduce myself . . . I am . . . |
| **Voici mon fils/mon mari/ma femme.** | Here is my son/my husband/my wife. |
| **Enchanté\* de faire votre connaissance.** | Pleased to meet you. |
| **C'est vous, . . . ?/Vous êtes . . . ?** | Are you . . . ? |
| **Oui, c'est moi.** | Yes, it's me. |
| **Oui/Non** | Yes/No |

  \* **Enchantée** for a woman.

### Saying goodbye

| Au revoir. | Good-bye. |
| A bientôt. | See you soon. |
| A tout à l'heure. | See you later. |
| A plus tard. | See you later. |

### Saying please and thank you

| S'il vous plaît | Please |
| Merci. | Thank you. |
| Merci beaucoup. | Thank you very much. |
| De rien. | You're welcome. |
| Il n'y a pas de quoi. | Don't mention it. |

## USEFUL WORDS AND PHRASES

| Donnez-moi la valise. | Give me the suitcase. |
| La voiture est là-bas. | The car is over there. |
| L'hôtel est tout près. | The hotel is nearby. |
| Vous avez fait un bon voyage? | Did you have a good trip? |
| Dépêchons-nous, maman! | Let's hurry, Mom! |
| Le taxi attend. | The taxi is waiting. |
| Eh bien | Well |
| Prends les bagages. | Take the luggage. |

La famille (the family)
les Bergeron (the Bergerons)
les parents
le grand-père | la grand-mère
Henri (le père)
Agathe (la mère)
les enfants
Julien (le fils)
Fabienne (la fille)

## the way it works

### People and things

In French, words for both people and things are masculine or feminine. There is no sure way of guessing which is which, and the gender of each noun must simply be learned. The word for "the" is **le** before a masculine noun—**le fils, le taxi**—and **la** before a feminine noun—**la voiture, la valise**. Use **l'** before masculine and feminine words beginning with a vowel and most words beginning with h: **l'arrivée, l'hôtel**.

For more than one thing use **les**—**les bagages, les passagers**.

If you want to say "a" in French, use **un** before a masculine noun—**un voyage, un départ**—and **une** before a feminine noun—**une valise, une traversée**.

### I am, you are

| **Je suis** Patrick Vincent. | I am Patrick Vincent. |
| **Vous êtes** M. Vincent. | You are Mr. Vincent. |

The word for "you" in French is normally **vous**, but with people you know well and with members of the family and children, use the word **tu**.
**Tu es** = you are (familiar)

3

## Mine and yours

To say "my" in French, use **mon** for a masculine noun—**mon fils, mon sac**; and **ma** for a feminine noun—**ma fille, ma sœur**. For words in the plural, "my" is **mes**: **mes parents, mes compliments**.

To say "your" in French, use **votre** for singular masculine and feminine nouns—**votre frère, votre sœur**; and **vos** for nouns in the plural—**vos bagages, vos enfants**. However, when talking to members of the family or close friends use **ton, ta** or **tes** instead of **votre**: **ton frère, ta sœur, tes parents**.

Note: for masculine and feminine nouns beginning with a vowel or **h** use **mon, ton**: **mon arrivée, ton hôtel**.

The full list of possessive adjectives is on p. 10.

## things to do

**1.1** Practice saying hello and goodbye to the following people, not forgetting to add **monsieur, madame, mademoiselle** as appropriate.

1 Mr. Dupont (a business colleague)

2 Mrs. Le Gros (a shopkeeper)

3 Mrs. Maury (a friend of your mother)

4 Clothilde (a waitress)

5 Damien (a friend)

**1.2** Complete the following exchanges in which meetings are taking place:

1 Mme Leclerc:   Bonjour madame. Vous êtes Madame Valéry?
  Mme Valéry:   Oui . . .
2 Employé:   Bonjour monsieur/madame. Votre nom, s'il vous plaît?
  Vous:
3 Mme Ricard:   Je me présente. Je suis Madame Ricard.
  Vous:
4 Mme Maury:   Bonjour Robert. Comment allez-vous?
  Robert:
5 Antoine:   Salut André! Comment ca va?
  André:

**1.3** Is it yours? Reply, saying, "Yes it is." Use **mon, ma** or **mes**.
1 C'est votre valise, monsieur?
2 C'est votre taxi, madame?
3 C'est votre voiture, madame?
4 C'est votre fils, monsieur?
5 C'est votre nom, monsieur?
6 Ce sont vos bagages, madame?
7 C'est votre passeport, monsieur?

## RESERVING ACCOMMODATIONS

**Accommodations**    There are five categories of hotel, with a rating of up to four stars. Prices are posted up in the **réception** and on the backs of the bedroom doors, and are usually quoted for two—although prices may be the same irrespective of the number of occupants. Prices do not usually include breakfast. Hotel guests may be asked to fill out a registration form (**une fiche**) on arrival, giving details of nationality, passport number, and so on. **Pensions** are similar to boarding houses, and **auberges** to country inns. **Logis de France** are reasonably priced country hotels, and **relais de campagne** are more expensive country inns. The tourist office (**le syndicat d'initiative**) in each town keeps a list of hotels as well as rooms in private homes.

**Gîtes de France** offer cheap self-catering accommodations outside the cities and are extremely popular.

Youth hostels (**Auberges de jeunesse**) are also very popular in summer, when it is essential to reserve in advance. Details of maximum length of stay, which may be only 3 days or up to a week, are available from the International Youth Hostel Handbook.

## à l'hôtel/at the hotel

Patrick and Bernard check in at the hotel. Patrick has reserved a room.

| | |
|---|---|
| Réceptionniste: | Bonjour, messieurs. |
| Patrick: | Bonjour, Madame. **J'ai réservé une chambre pour deux nuits**. |
| Réceptionniste: | Oui, monsieur. C'est à quel nom? |
| Patrick: | **Au nom de M. Vincent.** |
| Réceptionniste: | Ah oui, M. Vincent. Votre chambre est le numéro neuf au deuxième étage. Voulez-vous remplir cette fiche, s'il vous plaît? |
| Patrick: | Oui, madame, volontiers. |
| (He fills in the form.) | |
| Réceptionniste: | Merci, monsieur. Voilà votre clé. |

Bernard, whose wife Martine (a teacher) is joining him later in the day, also wants a room for the night, but he hasn't reserved in advance.

| | |
|---|---|
| Bernard: | Moi aussi, **je voudrais une chambre pour ce soir**, s'il vous plaît, madame. |
| Réceptionniste: | Oui, monsieur. Pour combien de personnes? |
| Bernard: | **Pour deux personnes.** |
| Réceptionniste: | Il y a une très belle chambre à deux lits avec salle de bains au premier étage . . . Nous avons aussi une petite chambre à un grand lit avec douche au troisième étage. |
| Bernard: | Bon, alors la chambre avec salle de bains, **c'est combien?** |
| Réceptionniste: | Le prix de la chambre est de 500 francs, monsieur. |
| Bernard: | **Mais c'est trop cher!** Je prends la petite chambre. |
| Réceptionniste: | Très bien, monsieur. Voici la clé. C'est le numéro treize . . . |

**Camping**   Camping is only permitted at officially designated sites, lists of which can be obtained from the French Government Tourist Office, as well as the various handbooks. Campgrounds have a one- to four-star rating, and the larger ones have many amenities, such as restaurants, supermarkets, heated pools and sports facilities. Tents, trailers, and cabins can be rented at many sites. Camping is very popular, and it is essential to reserve well in advance for the summer months.

## au camping/at the campground

The Bergeron family are taking Claire camping with them. They arrive at the campground where they have reserved a spot. Henri Bergeron, the father, is talking to the campground manager.

| | |
|---|---|
| Henri: | Bonjour, monsieur. Je suis M. Bergeron. **J'ai réservé un emplacement pour huit jours.** |
| Gardien: | Oui, monsieur. Votre emplacement est là-bas, sous ces arbres. La piscine est à côté. |
| Agathe B.: | Mais c'est parfait! Nous dressons les tentes tout de suite, les enfants . . . |
| Henri: | Julien, où est le réchaud? |
| Julien: | Je ne sais pas, papa. Il n'est pas dans la voiture. |
| Henri: | Ah non! J'ai laissé le réchaud à la maison. |
| Agathe: | Qu'est-ce qu'il y a, chéri? Tu ne trouves pas le réchaud? Quelle tête en l'air! Ça ne fait rien, ce soir nous achetons des plats cuisinés! |

### Getting a room at a hotel

| | |
|---|---|
| Chambres à louer | Rooms for rent |
| J'ai réservé une chambre. | I have reserved a room. |
| Vous avez une chambre libre? | Do you have a room free? |
| Je voudrais une chambre . . . | I would like a room . . . |
|   pour ce soir |   for this evening |
|   pour le weekend |   for the weekend |
|   pour deux nuits |   for two nights |
|   pour huit jours   } <br>   pour une semaine |   for a week |
|   à un lit/à deux lits/à un grand lit |   with single bed/twin beds/double bed |
|   avec salle de bains/douche/ <br>    cabinet de toilette (WC)/balcon |   with a bathroom/shower/toilet/ <br>    balcony |
|   au rez-de-chaussée |   on the first floor |
|   au premier étage |   on the second floor |
| C'est à quel nom? | What name is it? |
| C'est au nom de . . . | It's in the name of . . . |
| Pour combien de personnes? | For how many? |
| Votre chambre est le numéro neuf. | Your room is no. 9. |
| Voulez-vous remplir cette fiche? | Will you fill out this form? |
| chambre d'hôte | bed and breakfast |
| en pension/en demi-pension | full board/half board |
| la réception | reception |
| l'escalier/l'ascenseur | stairs/elevator |
| Il y a une très belle chambre. | There's a very nice room. |
| Nous avons aussi une petite chambre. | We also have a small room. |
| Puis-je voir la chambre? | Can I see the room? |

## At the hotel

| | |
|---|---|
| La clé du (cinq), s'il vous plaît. | The key to room (five), please. |
| Voilà votre clé. | Here's your key. |
| Puis-je avoir un oreiller?/du savon? | Can I have a pillow?/some soap? |
| une serviette de bain? | a bath towel? |
| encore une couverture? | another blanket? |
| La lumière ne marche pas. | The light doesn't work. |
| La douche . . . | The shower . . . |
| La note, s'il vous plaît. | The bill, please. |
| Est-ce que le service est compris? | Is service included? |
| Je crois qu'il y a une erreur. | I think there is a mistake. |

## Reserving a campsite

| | |
|---|---|
| Est-ce qu'il y a un camping près d'ici? | Is there a campground near here? |
| Avez-vous un emplacement? | Do you have a free site? |
| J'ai réservé un emplacement. | I have reserved a site. |
| Votre emplacement est là-bas | Your site is over there |
| . . . sous ces arbres. | . . . under those trees. |
| La piscine est à côté. | The swimming pool is nearby. |
| C'est pour une tente/pour une caravane. | It's for a tent/for a trailer. |
| C'est combien par nuit? | How much is it per night? |
| Y a-t-il de l'eau potable? | Is there drinking water? |
| un magasin sur place? | a shop on the site? |
| un restaurant?/une laverie? | a restaurant?/a laundry? |
| une piscine? | a swimming pool? |
| Nous dressons les tentes tout de suite. | We'll put up the tents at once. |
| Nous achetons des plats cuisinés. | We'll buy carryout food. |

## Prices

| | |
|---|---|
| C'est combien? | How much is it? |
| Quel est le tarif? | What are the rates? |
| Quel est le prix de la chambre? | What is the price of the room? |
| Le prix est de . . . | The price is . . . |
| C'est trop cher! | It's too expensive! |
| Je prends la petite chambre. | I'll take the little room. |

## USEFUL WORDS AND PHRASES

| | |
|---|---|
| volontiers | of course, willingly |
| Bon, alors | Good (then) |
| Voici . . . | Here is |
| C'est parfait! | It's perfect! |
| Où est le réchaud? | Where is the stove? |
| Je ne sais pas. | I don't know. |
| Il n'est pas dans la voiture. | It isn't in the car. |
| J'ai laissé . . . à la maison. | I have left . . . at home. |
| Qu'est-ce qu'il y a, chéri? | What's the matter, darling? |
| Tu ne trouves pas . . . ? | Can't you find . . . ? |
| Ça ne fait rien. | It doesn't matter. |
| Quelle tête en l'air! | What a scatterbrain! |

## Camping signs

| | |
|---|---|
| location de tentes | tent rental |
| eau potable | drinking water |
| bloc sanitaire | washhouse |
| défense de laver la vaisselle dans les lavabos | no dish washing in the sinks |
| parking obligatoire | compulsory parking |
| réservé aux caravanes | trailers only |
| interdiction de camper ici | no camping here |
| caravaning interdit | no trailers allowed |
| complet | full |

CAMPING "DES SABLES DORES"

rue du Port, S. JEAN-SUR-MER

Terrain ouvert du 13 mai au 30 septembre.
Possibilité de réservation.

Bureau de réception
**Camp office**

Camp gardé
**Camp supervised**

Branchement électrique pour caravanes
**Electricity hookups for trailers**

Prises pour rasoirs électriques
**Outlets for electric razors**

Eau chaude pour douches
**Hot water for showers**

Lavoirs
**Washhouses**

Table à repasser
**Ironing table**

Ping-pong
**Table tennis**

Balançoire
**Swing**

Piscine
**Swimming pool**

Distribution du courrier
**Postal service**

Dépot de camping gaz
**Propane gas on sale**

Ravitaillement au camp
**Stores at the camp**

**DISTANCES**
Restaurant à 500 m
Plage des sables dorés à 4 km
Canotage, voile ou yachting 3 km 500

Ecole équitation à 1 km
Pêche en rivière à 200 m du camp
Casino, cinéma, tennis à 3 km

## the way it works

### At

The word for "at" in French is **à**: **à Paris**. Its form changes depending on whether it is followed by a masculine, feminine or plural noun: **au restaurant**, **à la maison**, **aux magasins**. Before a noun beginning with a vowel or **h** use **à l'**: **à l'hôtel** (at the hotel).

## This and that

The word for "this" or "that" is **ce** for a masculine word (**ce soir** = this evening), **cette** for a feminine word (**cette fiche** = this form), **cet** for a masculine word beginning with a vowel or **h** (**cet arbre** = this tree, **cet hôtel** = this hotel), and **ces** for a word in the plural (**ces arbres** = these trees).

## It is

**C'est** means "it is": **c'est trop cher** = it's too expensive. But if you are talking about something in particular, use **il** or **elle** for that thing: **il est dans la voiture**, it (e.g., the stove) is in the car.

## I, you, he, etc. (subject pronouns)

Here is a complete list of the subject pronouns:

| | | | |
|---|---|---|---|
| I | **je** | we | **nous** |
| you (singular) | **tu** | you (plural) | **vous** |
| he/it | **il** | they | **ils** |
| she/it | **elle** | they | **elles** |

## His, her, its, etc. (possessive adjectives)

The complete list is as follows:

| *masc.* | *fem.* | *pl.* | | *masc.* | *fem.* | *pl.* | |
|---|---|---|---|---|---|---|---|
| **mon** | **ma** | **mes** | my | **notre** | **notre** | **nos** | our |
| **ton** | **ta** | **tes** | your (familiar) | **votre** | **votre** | **vos** | your |
| **son** | **sa** | **ses** | his/her/its | **leur** | **leur** | **leurs** | their |

## Verbs

The verb **trouver** means "to find," and many French verbs have endings like **trouver**. It is worth spending some time learning these endings.

| | | | |
|---|---|---|---|
| je trouv**e** | I find | nous trouv**ons** | we find |
| tu trouv**es** | you find | vous trouv**ez** | you find |
| il trouv**e** | he, it finds | ils trouv**ent** | they find (masc.) |
| elle trouv**e** | she, it finds | elles trouv**ent** | they find (fem.) |

Remember to use the **tu** form of "you" when speaking to a child or close friend, and the **vous** form when speaking to someone you don't know or more than one person.

## Adjectives

Adjectives in French change their endings depending on whether the noun is masculine or feminine:
**un petit lit** = a small bed BUT **une petite chambre** = a small room
**un grand camping** = a big campsite BUT **une grande tente** = a big tent

## Negatives

If you want to say "No, it isn't," "No I don't," etc., simply put **ne** before the verb and **pas** after the verb:

| | |
|---|---|
| Je **ne** sais **pas**. | I don't know. |
| Il **n**'est **pas** dans la voiture. | It isn't in the car. |

**4** Practice reserving different sorts of hotel rooms.

1    Je voudrais une
     chambre avec . . .

2    Je voudrais . . .

3    Je voudrais . . .

4    Je voudrais . . .

5    Je voudrais . . .

6    Je voudrais . . .

Now practice reserving for your friend who wants a room with a lot of extras (double bed, shower, and toilet). Elle voudrait . . .

**5** Where are the following objects? You think they are in the obvious place.

1 Où est le réchaud? Dans la voiture?
  Oui, le réchaud est dans la voiture.
2 Où est la valise? Dans le coffre? (trunk of car)
3 Où est la clé? Dans la porte? (door)
4 Où est la tente? Sous les arbres?
5 Où est la douche? Dans la salle de bains?
6 Où est le passeport? Dans le sac? (bag)

**6** But none of these things is where you thought it was. This time use **il** or **elle** for "it."

1 Le réchaud? Non, il n'est pas dans la voiture.
2 La valise? Non, elle . . .
3 La clé? Non, elle . . .
4 La tente? Non, elle . . .
5 La douche? Non, elle . . .
6 Le passeport? Non, il . . .

**7** Will everything fit in the car? Your friends are anxious to know if your belongings will take up too much room. You reassure them.

1 Tu as une grande tente?
  Non, elle est petite.
2 Tu as une grande valise?
  Non, . . .
3 Tu as un grand sac de couchage? (sleeping bag)
4 Tu as un grand réchaud?
5 Tu as un grand sac?

**8** You are with a group of people staying at a hotel.
Tell the others what room numbers they have been allocated, and on what floor. (See p. 80 for a list of numbers.)

1 Alexandre: room 7 on the third floor.
  Alexandre, vous avez la chambre numéro sept au troisième étage.
2 François: room 5 on the third floor
3 Nathalie: room 10 on the second floor.
4 Christian: room 2 on the first floor (au rez-de-chaussée).
5 Florence: room 14 on the fourth floor.

11

## ORDERING BREAKFAST

Breakfast in France is a light meal usually consisting of bread and butter, and sometimes croissants or rolls, and is served with freshly made coffee.

## le petit déjeuner à l'hôtel/breakfast at the hotel

Before setting out for the design exhibition in Paris, Patrick Vincent and Martine Rousseau are having breakfast in the hotel. Patrick calls the waiter.

| | |
|---|---|
| Patrick: | **Garçon, s'il vous plaît!** |
| | (he turns to Martine) Mais, où est Bernard? Il est déjà neuf heures. |
| Martine: | Il se renseigne sur le départ des trains pour Paris. |
| Garçon: | Vous prenez, monsieur-madame? |
| Martine: | **Moi, je prends un jus d'orange et un yaourt nature.** |
| Patrick: | **Et pour moi du thé, du pain et des croissants avec de la confiture.** Ah, voilà Bernard qui arrive . . . |
| Garçon; | (turns to Bernard) Et pour vous, monsieur? |
| Bernard: | **Apportez-moi un café noir, s'il vous plaît.** |
| Garçon: | C'est tout? Très bien, madame-messieurs. |
| Martine: | Le train pour Paris part à quelle heure? |
| Bernard: | Il faut se dépêcher, mes amis. Le train part dans une demi-heure. |

## Ordering breakfast

| | |
|---|---|
| Garçon, s'il vous plaît! | Waiter! |
| Vous prenez, monsieur-madame? | What would you like? |
| Moi, je prends un jus d'orange/un yaourt nature. | I'd like an orange juice/a plain yogurt. |
| Et pour moi . . . | And for me . . . |
| du thé/du café/du chocolat | tea/coffee/hot chocolate |
| du pain/des croissants | bread/croissants |
| avec de la confiture | with jam |
| et du beurre | and butter |
| Apportez-moi un café noir/un café au lait. | Bring me a black coffee/coffee with milk. |
| C'est tout? | Anything else? |
| Vous avez des croissants? | Do you have croissants? |

### USEFUL WORDS AND PHRASES

| | |
|---|---|
| déjà | already |
| Voilà (Bernard) qui arrive. | Here comes (Bernard). |
| Très bien | Very good |
| Il faut se dépêcher, mes amis. | We must hurry, my friends. |

# FRENCH RAILWAYS

**French Railways**   The *SNCF* (The French railroad company) runs a modern and efficient service. All the main railway lines radiate out from Paris. Types of trains include the following:

| | |
|---|---|
| TEE | Trans-Europ-Express. Fast international service, first-class only. |
| TGV | Train à grande vitesse. High-speed inter-city service. Selected routes. |
| Rapide | Fast, long-distance express linking main cities. |
| Express | Slower long-distance train. |
| Omnibus | Local stopping train. |
| Autorail | Short-haul diesel. |

Reserve in advance for long-distance trips and check the bargain fares available on certain days of the week. In general children under 4 travel free and under 10 travel at half fare. When you have bought your ticket, don't forget to validate (**composter**) it in the date-stamping machine at the entrance to the platform (see p. 16).

## au guichet/at the ticket window

Sylvie, a colleague of Bernard, is at the Rouen train station buying a ticket to Paris.

| | |
|---|---|
| Sylvie: | **Je voudrais un billet pour Paris, s'il vous plaît.** |
| Employé: | Oui, madame, un aller simple ou un aller-retour? |
| Sylvie: | **Un aller simple, s'il vous plaît.** |
| Employé: | En première ou seconde classe? |
| Sylvie: | **En seconde.** |
| Employé: | Voilà, madame, ça fait quatre-vingts francs. |
| Sylvie: | Merci, monsieur. Dites-moi, **à quelle heure part le prochain train?** |
| Employé: | A 12 h 17, madame. C'est le quai numéro 3. Vous avez juste cinq minutes! |

*A la gare (at the train station)*

| | |
|---|---|
| **Accès aux quais** | This way to platforms |
| **Consigne (automatique)** | Short-term baggage storage (lockers) |
| **Défense de fumer** | No smoking |
| **Départ** | Departures |
| **Arrivée** | Arrivals |
| **Bureau de renseignements** | Information office |
| **Salle d'attente** | Waiting room |
| **Grandes lignes** | Long-distance trains |
| **Trains de banlieue** | Suburban trains |
| **l'Horaire SNCF** | Train schedule |
| **Wagon-Restaurant** | Restaurant car |
| **Wagon-lit** | Sleeping car |

**DÉFENSE DE FUMER**

**WAGON-LIT**     **ARRIVÉE**

**DÉPART**     **QUAI 4**

### What time is it?

| | |
|---|---|
| Quelle heure est-il? | What time is it? |
| Il est neuf heures. | It's nine o'clock. |
| . . . neuf heures cinq | . . . five after nine |
| . . . neuf heures un (or et) quart | . . . a quarter after nine |
| . . . neuf heures et demie | . . . nine thirty |
| . . . neuf heures moins le quart | . . . a quarter to nine |
| . . . neuf heures moins dix | . . . ten to nine |
| du matin/de l'après-midi/du soir | in the morning/afternoon/evening |

... HEURES

... HEURES ET QUART

... HEURES MOINS LE QUART

... HEURES ET DEMIE

### Train information

| | |
|---|---|
| Renseignements | Information |
| Il se renseigne sur . . . | He is finding out about . . . |
| . . . le départ des trains pour Paris | . . . departure times of trains to Paris |
| Il part à quelle heure, le train pour Paris?/de Paris? | What time does the Paris train leave? |
| A quelle heure est le prochain train? | What time is the next train? |
| Il part a dix-sept heures quinze. | It leaves at 17:15. |
| . . . dans cinq minutes | . . . in five minutes |
| . . . dans une demi-heure | . . . in half an hour |
| . . . à midi/à minuit | . . . at noon/at midnight |
| Il faut combien de temps . . . ? | How long does it take . . . ? |
| . . . pour aller de Boulogne à Paris? | to go from Boulogne to Paris? |
| Il faut deux heures. | It takes two hours. |
| Il arrive à quelle heure? | When does it arrive? |
| Il arrive à . . . | It arrives at . . . |
| aujourd'hui/demain/hier | today/tomorrow/yesterday |
| C'est quelle ligne pour . . . ? | What train do you take for . . . ? |
| Est-ce qu'il y a une correspondance? | Do you have to change trains? |
| Non, c'est direct. | No, it's direct. |
| Oui, il faut changer à Vichy. | Yes, you have to change at Vichy. |

### Buying a ticket

| | |
|---|---|
| le guichet | ticket window |
| Je voudrais un billet. | I want a ticket. |
| pour Paris | for Paris |
| un aller simple/un aller-retour | a one-way/round-trip ticket |
| en première/deuxième classe | first/second class |
| le quai numéro trois | platform 3 |
| tarif réduit | reduced fare |
| la réservation | reservation |

*At the train station, listen for the following phrases in announcements:*

| | |
|---|---|
| le train en direction de/à destination de . . . | . . . the train for . . . |
| le train en provenance de . . . | the train from . . . |
| en retard/à l'avance | late/early |
| voie quatre | track 4 |

## USEFUL WORDS AND PHRASES

**Voilà**    There you are                **Dites-moi**    Tell me

## the way it works

### To make a noun plural

When talking about more than one thing, you use **les** instead of **le/la/l'** and
normally you add **s** to the noun:
le croissant; **les** croissant**s**
la valise; **les** valise**s**
l'heure; **les** heure**s**

However, a few nouns add **x** instead or change **-al** to **-aux**:
le château; les château**x** (castles), le journ**al**; les journ**aux** (newspapers).

### How to say "some" or "any"

Note the following phrase from the first dialogue: **Du** thé, **du** pain et **des** croissants,
avec **de la** confiture. If you want to say "some":
Use **du** with a masculine word:    **du** thé, **du** pain
    **de la** with a feminine word:    **de la** confiture
    **des** with a plural word:        **des** croissants
With a word starting with a vowel or **h**, use **de l'**: De l'eau, s'il vous plaît (Some
water, please).

## Telling the time

Always state the hour before the minutes.

**Il est trois heures dix.**          It is ten after three.
**Il est dix heures moins vingt.**    It is twenty to ten.

Official French time always uses the twenty-four hour clock.
**Il est treize heures (13h00).**      It is 13:00 hours (1:00 p.m.)
(**h** is short for **heures** but it is usually omitted in timetables.)

In less official use and in speech, use the twelve-hour clock.
To specify the time of day, you can add: **du matin/de l'après-midi/du soir**.

## Adverbs

In French most adverbs are formed by adding **-ment** to the feminine form of an adjective:
lente (slow)                          lente**ment** (slowly)
heureuse (happy)                      heureuse**ment** (happily)

## To be and to have

Here are two very common verbs which do not follow the normal patterns:
**être** *to be*

| je **suis** | I am | nous **sommes** | we are |
| tu **es** | you are | vous **êtes** | you are |
| il **est** | he, it is | ils **sont** | they are |
| elle **est** | she, it is | elles **sont** | they are |

**avoir** *to have*

| j'**ai** | I have | nous **avons** | we have |
| tu **as** | you have | vous **avez** | you have |
| il **a** | he, it has | ils **ont** | they have |
| elle **a** | she, it has | elles **ont** | they have |

## Asking questions

If you want to ask a question there are several ways of doing it in French:
Vous avez des œufs.                    You have some eggs.
Vous avez des œufs? (*with questioning tone*)
Avez-vous des œufs?                    Do you have any eggs?
Est-ce que vous avez des œufs?

## *things to do*

**2.1** The waiter is taking orders for breakfast.
Vous prenez, messieurs-dames?
Each member of your party wants something different.
What might they say?
Example: Denise:   Je voudrais du café.

**1** Catherine:   **2** Lucien:   **3** Nadine:

**4** Olivier:   **5** André:

**2.2** *Quelle heure est-il?* Someone asks you the time. But it seems that the watches of each member of your party say different times, e.g., Il est trois heures.

**1**   **2**   **3**   **4**   **5**   **6**

**2.3** *Au guichet des reinseignements*/At the information window
You overhear the ticket agent advising a passenger about trains. Can you guess what the passenger is asking?

Passenger:  . . . . . . . . . . . . . . . . . . . . . . . . . . . . . . . . . . . . . . . . . . . . . . . . . . . . . . . . .
Agent:      Le prochain train pour Paris part à neuf heures trente.
Passenger:  . . . . . . . . . . . . . . . . . . . . . . . . . . . . . . . . . . . . . . . . . . . . . . . . . . . . . . . . .
Agent:      Il faut environ deux heures et demie por aller de Boulogne à Paris.
Passenger:  . . . . . . . . . . . . . . . . . . . . . . . . . . . . . . . . . . . . . . . . . . . . . . . . . . . . . . . . .
Agent:      Il arrive à onze heurs cinquante-cinq.
Passenger:  . . . . . . . . . . . . . . . . . . . . . . . . . . . . . . . . . . . . . . . . . . . . . . . . . . . . . . . . .
Agent:      Non, c'est direct.

**2.4** Buying a ticket. You are at a ticket office in Paris with a party of tourists, several of whom want to go to different places. Since you are the only one who speaks French, you have to buy the tickets. The first one is done for you.

**1**  Katy: *Round-trip ticket to Vichy, second class.* Elle voudrait un billet aller-retour à Vichy, en deuxième classe.
**2**  Mike: *One-way to Lyon, first class.*
**3**  Stuart and Alison: *Round-trip to Avignon, second class.* (Ils voudraient . . .)
**4**  Peter: *Round-trip to Bordeaux, second class.*
**5**  John and Sue: *One-way to Nice, first class.*

# TRAVELING BY PUBLIC TRANSPORTATION

**Le métro**   The subway in Paris is called the **Métro**. It is a cheap way to travel in Paris and the network is very extensive (see map). In the city you pay a flat fare however many stations you travel. If you are using the service a lot, it is worth buying a book of tickets, called a **carnet**, and, for short visits it is worth finding out about a special tourist ticket (**billet de tourisme**) valid for up to a week, which you can use on most other forms of public transportation as well.

## dans le métro/in the metro

Patrick and Bernard have arrived in Paris. They want to go to the Paris-Nord Convention Center at Roissy and look at the metro map to find out how to get there.

Patrick:   **Pour aller à l'Exposition**, voyons . . .

Bernard:   Regardons le plan du métro. **Nous prenons le RER direction Roissy**, et **nous descendons au Parc des Expositions**.

Martine:   Vous allez passer tout l'après-midi à Roissy?

Barnard:   Oui, bien sûr. L'exposition ouvre demain matin et nous devons rencontrer des collègues.

Martine:    Bon. Dans ce cas-là, je vous laisse, mes amis. Moi, je vais rejoindre une amie, et après je vais dans les grands magasins. Je cherche de nouvelles chaussures et une jupe, et à Paris—il faut en profiter.

Bernard:    Alors, chérie, n'oublie pas d'acheter des petits cadeaux pour les enfants.

## *Traveling on the métro*

| | |
|---|---|
| Où se trouve la station de métro? | Where is the subway station? |
| Regardons le plan du métro. | Let's look at the metro map. |
| Prenons le RER. | We'll take the RER. |
| direction Roissy | going to Roissy |
| Nous descendons au Parc des Expositions. | We get off at Convention Center. |
| un ticket (de métro) | subway ticket |
| un carnet de tickets | book of tickets |

**Le RER**   The newest and fastest means of crossing Paris, this network consists of three lines and extends outwards to the suburbs. Although the flat fare system applies as on the métro in the middle of Paris, fares do vary according to the length of journey into the suburbs.

**L'autobus**   For information about bus service, go to the local tourist office or bus station. On most buses you pay as you enter, and you will probably have to stand because there is not a great deal of sitting space. If you have bought a **carnet** of tickets be prepared to use several tickets for one journey, as fares are not standard.

**Le taxi**   To find a taxi go to a taxi stand. There are often set fares between main train stations. You should expect to have to pay a set charge for you and your luggage (**la prise en charge**) and to give a tip (**un pourboire**) of 10–15% to the driver.

## FINDING YOUR WAY

## pour aller à la plage?/how do we get to the beach?

Julien and Claire want to go to the beach. They ask a policeman (**un gendarme**) the best way to get there.

Julien: **Excusez-moi, monsieur, la plage c'est loin d'ici?**
Gendarme: Non, c'est tout près; vous avez dix minutes à pied. Attendez, je vais vous montrer sur le plan. Nous sommes ici, n'est-ce pas? Vous tournez à gauche dans la rue du Port. Vous continuez tout droit et à cent mètres vous prenez la petite rue à droite, la rue de la Plage . . .
Julien: . . . mais, c'est trop difficile. **Est-ce qu'il y a un autobus?**
Gendarme: Oui, l'arrêt d'autobus est juste en face du camping. Mais les bus ne sont pas très fréquents. Ils passent toutes les deux heures.
Claire: Bon, moi **je vais à la plage à pied**. Tu viens avec moi, Julien?
Julien: Non. Allons demander à Papa de nous y emmener en voiture.
Claire: Comme tu es paresseux!

### How do I get there?

| | |
|---|---|
| **Excusez-moi, monsieur . . .** | Excuse me, sir . . . |
| **la plage c'est loin d'ici?** | is the beach far from here? |
| **Pour aller à . . . ?** | How do I get to . . . ? |
| **Où est . . . Où se trouve . . . ?** | Where is . . . ? |
| **Pardon, monsieur, le (terrain de) camping?** | Excuse me, where is the campground? |
| **C'est loin d'ici?** | Is it far from here? |

| | |
|---|---|
| Non, c'est tout près. | No, it's very near. |
| c'est assez près/assez loin | it's quite near/quite far |
| Je vous montre sur le plan. | I'll show you on the map. |
| Nous sommes ici. | We are here. |
| Vous tournez à gauche/à droite. | Turn left/right. |
| la rue du Port | Harbor Street |
| Continuez tout droit. | Go straight ahead. |
| Allez tout droit. | |
| à cent mètres | after 100 meters |
| Vous prenez la petite rue à droite. | Take the little street on the right. |
| jusqu'à | as far as |
| C'est juste en face. | It's right across the street. |
| Prenez la première rue à gauche. | Take the first street on the left. |
| C'est la troisième rue à droite. | It's the third street on the right. |
| Vous avez vingt minutes à pied. | It's 20 minutes on foot. |
| Est-ce qu'il y a un autobus? | Is there a bus? |
| L'arrêt d'autobus est juste en face. | The bus stop is just across the street. |
| Les bus ne sont pas très fréquents. | The buses are not very frequent. |
| Ils passent toutes les deux heures. | They pass every two hours. |
| Vous pouvez y aller | You can get there |
| par le train/en autobus | by train/by bus |
| par le métro/par avion | by subway/by plane |
| en taxi/en auto | by taxi/by car |
| à bicyclette/en vélo | on a bike |
| Je vais à pied. | I'm going on foot. |

## USEFUL WORDS AND PHRASES (Dialogue 1)

| | |
|---|---|
| tout l'après-midi | all afternoon |
| bien sûr | of course |
| rencontrer | to meet |
| L'Exposition ouvre | the exhibition opens |
| Nous devons rencontrer des collègues. | We have to meet some colleagues. |
| rejoindre | to meet up with |
| dans ce ca-là | in that case |
| je vous laisse | I'll leave you |
| les grands magasins | department stores |
| Je cherche de nouvelles chaussures. | I'm looking for some new shoes. |
| il faut en profiter | we must take advantage of it |
| Alors, chérie | Well, my love |
| n'oublie pas d'acheter des cadeaux | don't forget to buy some presents |
| pour les enfants | for the children |

## USEFUL WORDS AND PHRASES (Dialogue 2)

| | |
|---|---|
| trop difficile | too difficult |
| Tu viens avec moi? | Are you coming with me? |
| Allons demander à Papa . . . | Let's ask Dad . . . |
| . . . de nous y emmener | . . . to take us there |
| Comme tu es paresseux! | You're so lazy! |

première à
gauche

tout droit

deuxième à
droite

## the way it works

**De** (= of)

The word for "of" in French is **de**. I is used like this:
la valise **de** Claire (Claire's suitcase).
Use **du** before a masculine noun:
le plan **du** Métro (the map of the metro).
Use **de la** before a feminine noun:
la voiture **de la** dame (the lady's car).
Use **de l'** before a word beginning with a vowel or **h**:
le prix **de l'**emplacement (the price of the site).
Use **des** before a plural noun:
le départ **des** trains (the departure of the trains).
la chambre **des** touristes (the visitors' room).

Office
de
Tourisme

Note: **de** also has other functions. It can, for example, mean "from" and "to." It is
often used as a link-word, as in the following examples:
à côté **de** (beside, next to): à côté **du** restaurant
près **de** (near): près **de la** mer
en face **de** (across from): en face **de l'**hôtel

## Adjectives

Most adjectives in French come after the noun: un yaourt **nature**, un café **noir**. However, some very common ones come before the noun. Here are some common adjectives which have unusual endings:

*beau/belle* fine, lovely, beautiful etc.

| | |
|---|---|
| le **beau** garçon    le **bel** homme | la **belle** chambre |
| les **beaux** chiens | les **belles** photos |

*nouveau/nouvelle* new

| | |
|---|---|
| le **nouveau** sac    le **nouvel** ami | la **nouvelle** valise |
| les **nouveaux** projets | les **nouvelles** chaussures |

*vieux/vieille* old

| | |
|---|---|
| le **vieux** château    le **vieil** hôtel | la **vieille** femme |
| les **vieux** jardins | les **vieilles** tentes |

Adjectives mostly take an **s** in the plural: les petit**s** garçons. If the noun is feminine they mostly take **es**: les grand**es** maisons.

Notice that when you want to say "some," with many adjectives (particularly feminine ones) which precede the noun, you sometimes use **de** instead of **des**: de nouvelles chaussures.

## How to use the verb **aller** (to go)

Note the following phrases from the dialogues:

| | |
|---|---|
| Pour **aller** à l'Exposition? | To get to the Exhibition? |
| **Vous allez** passer tout l'après-midi . . .? | Will you spend all afternoon . . .? |
| **Je vais** à pied. | I'm going on foot. |

These are examples of the verb **aller** (to go) which is also used as a way of expressing the simple future tense, as in English (**Je vais** rejoindre une amie = *I'm going* to meet a friend). Here is the present tense:

| | | | |
|---|---|---|---|
| je **vais** | I go | nous **allons** | we go |
| tu **vas** | you go | vous **allez** | you go |
| il/elle **va** | he/she/it goes | ils/elles **vont** | they go |

## How do I get to . . .?

There are several ways of asking for directions in French. Here are some of them.

| | |
|---|---|
| **Où est** la poste, s'il vous plaît? | Where is the post office, please? |
| **Est-ce qu'il y a** une boulangerie **près d'ici**? | Is there a bakery near here? |
| **Pour aller à** la plage, s'il vous plaît? | How do I get to the beach? |
| or simply | |
| S'il vous plaît, monsieur, l'Hôtel de la Plage? | The Beach Hotel, please? |

## things to do

**5** You want to go to the following places. Find different ways of asking for directions.

| | | | |
|---|---|---|---|
| (**a**) train station | (**d**) Harbor Street | (**f**) metro | (**i**) bus stop |
| (**b**) park | (**e**) post office | (**g**) beach | (**j**) bakery (la |
| (**c**) restaurant | (la poste) | (**h**) hotel | boulangerie) |

**2.6** Marie-Françoise is at the bus stop shown on the map and various passersby ask her for directions. Can you figure out from her instructions where it is that each of them wants to go to?

1 Continuez tout droit dans la rue Principale, et prenez la première à gauche. Puis, c'est la deuxième à gauche, et c'est sur votre droite.

2 Vous tournez à gauche dans la rue du Roi et vous prenez la première à droite. C'est à deux cents mètres, au coin de la rue.

3 C'est à côté de la mairie, juste en face du commissariat. Vous avez deux minutes à pied!

4 Longez la rue Principale, prenez la deuxième à gauche, et c'est le grand bâtiment (building) à gauche.

5 Continuez tout droit, puis c'est la deuxième rue à droite. C'est au coin, en face du petit café.

6 Tournez dans la rue du Roi et prenez la deuxième rue à gauche. Traversez la place et montez la côte. C'est juste en face, à côté du restaurant.

| | | | |
|---|---|---|---|
| l'arrêt d'autobus *bus stop* | la colline *hill* | le magasin *shop* | le stade *stadium* |
| la banque *bank* | le commissariat de police *police station* | la mairie *town hall* | le supermarché *supermarket* |
| la bibliothèque *library* | l'école *school* | le musée *museum* | le syndicat d'initiative *tourist information office* |
| la cabine téléphonique *phone booth* | l'église *church* | le parc *park* | |
| | les feux *traffic lights* | la piscine *swimming pool* | |
| le cinéma *movie theater* | la gare *station* | la place *square* | le théâtre *theater* |
| le cirque *circus* | l'hôpital *hospital* l'hôtel de ville *town hall* | la poste *post office* le restaurant *restaurant* | |

## SHOPPING FOR CLOTHES, ETC.
### *Sizes, colors, materials*

**Shopping**   Normal shopping hours are between 9 a.m. and about 6:30–7:30 p.m. Department stores are open all day but smaller shops often close for lunch between noon and 2 p.m. Many shops are closed on Mondays either for all or part of the day, but some food stores, particularly bakeries, are open on Sunday mornings. Supermarkets are sometimes open till 9 or 10 p.m.

## aux grands magasins/at the department store

Martine goes to a department store to look for a skirt.

Vendeuse:   Vous désirez, madame?
Martine:    **Je voudrais une jupe** . . . Ah! **Cette jupe bleue est jolie, mais elle est trop grande,** je pense . . . **Avez-vous la taille au-dessous?**
Vendeuse:   Quelle taille faites-vous, madame?
Martine:    **Du quarante.**

27

| | |
|---|---|
| Vendeuse: | Attendez, je vais voir . . . Non, je regrette . . . Mais cette jupe verte est jolie aussi, madame, et la noire fait très chic. La couleur est très à la mode cette année. |
| Martine: | Oui, c'est vrai. **Je préfère la noire. Vous avez la taille quarante en noir?** |
| Vendeuse: | Oui, madame, la voici. Vous voulez l'essayer? |
| (Martine tries it on) | |
| Vendeuse: | Ça fait très élègant, madame. |
| Martine: | Oui, **elle me plaît. Je la prends.** |

### *Buying clothes*

| | |
|---|---|
| **Vous désirez . . .?** | What would you like? |
| **Je voudrais une jupe.** | I want a skirt. |
| **Cette jupe bleue est jolie.** | This blue skirt is pretty. |
| **Elle est trop grande.** | It is too big. |
| **Il est trop grand/petit/long/court.** | It is too big/small/long/short. |
| **Avez-vous la taille au-dessous?/au-dessus?** | Have you got a size smaller?/bigger? |
| **Avez-vous quelque chose de plus petit?/de plus grand?/de moins cher?** | Have you anything smaller?/bigger?/cheaper? |
| **Quelle taille faites-vous?** | What is your size? |
| **Du quarante.** | (I wear a) 40. (*see sizes chart*) |
| **Ça fait très chic/très élégant.** | It's very chic/elegant. |
| **La couleur est très à la mode.** | The color is very fashionable. |
| **Je préfère la noire.** | I prefer the black one. |
| **Vous avez la taille quarante?** | Do you have a size 40? |
| **en noir** | in black |
| **Vous voulez l'essayer?** | Do you want to try it on? |
| **Je peux l'essayer?** | Can I try it on? |
| **Le style vous va bien.** | The style suits you. |
| **Il ne me va pas.** | It doesn't suit me. |
| **Je prendrais plutôt . . .** | I'd rather have . . . |
| **C'est vraiment difficile de choisir!** | It is so difficult to choose! |
| **Quelle couleur désirez-vous?** | What color would you like? |
| **Pouvez-vous me montrer une autre couleur?** | Can you show me another color? |
| **Attendez, je vais voir.** | Wait, I'll go and see. |
| **Non, je regrette . . .** | No, I'm sorry . . . |
| **Il/Elle coûte combien?** | How much is it? |
| **Il/Elle me plaît.** | I like it. |
| **Je le/la prends.** | I'll take it. |
| **C'est trop cher.** | It's too expensive. |
| **bon marché** | cheap |
| **Pouvez-vous l'emballer?** | Could you wrap it? |

## Shoes

| | |
|---|---|
| Quelle pointure faites-vous? | What shoe size are you? |
| (Je fais du) trente-huit. | I'm a 38. (*see sizes chart*) |
| une paire de chaussures | a pair of shoes |
| Elles sont très confortables. | They are very comfortable. |
| Elles me plaisent | I like them. |
| les sandales (f) | sandals |

### Clothes sizes—women

| U.S. | 4 | 6 | 8 | 10 | 12 | 14 | 16 |
|---|---|---|---|---|---|---|---|
| French | 38 | 40 | 42 | 44 | 46 | 48 | 50 |

### Collar sizes—men (approximate)

| U.S. | 14 | 14½ | 15 | 15½ | 16 | 16½ | 17 |
|---|---|---|---|---|---|---|---|
| French | 36 | 37 | 38 | 39/40 | 41 | 42 | 43 |

### Shoe sizes

| U.S. | 5 | 6 | 7 | 8 | 9 | 10 | 11 | 12 | 13 | 14 |
|---|---|---|---|---|---|---|---|---|---|---|
| French | 35 | 36 | 37 | 38 | 39 | 40 | 41 | 42 | 43 | 44 |

## Some common shops

| | | | |
|---|---|---|---|
| la papeterie | stationery store | la quincaillerie | hardware store |
| la pharmacie | pharmacy | la droguerie | household, hardware store |
| le magasin de chaussures | shoe store | le coiffeur | hair salon |
| la librairie | bookstore | le bureau de tabac | tobacco store |
| le marchand de journaux | newsstand | la bijouterie | jewelry store |

## au magasin de camping/at the camping shop

Henri needs a propane gas cylinder and has also forgotten to bring some essential camping items:

Vendeur: Vous désirez, monsieur?
Henri: **Je vourdrais une bouteille de camping gaz**, s'il vous plaît.
Vendeur: Oui, monsieur. Voilà. Vous désirez autre chose?
Henri: **J'ai besoin d'un tire-bouchon** . . . et aussi d'un ouvre-boîte.
Vendeur: Un ouvre-boîte comment? Montrez-moi.
Henri: (Points to a shelf) Comme ça.
Vendeur: C'est tout? Alors, ça fait quarante-cinq francs, monsieur.

### *At the camping supply store*

| | |
|---|---|
| **une bouteille de camping gaz** | a cylinder of propane gas |
| **Vous désirez autre chose?** | Anything else? |
| **J'ai besoin de** | I need |
| **un tire-bouchon** | a corkscrew |
| **un ouvre-boît** | a can opener |
| **. . . comment?** | . . . what kind? |
| **montrez-moi** | show me |
| **comme ça** | like that |

### *Colors*

| | | | |
|---|---|---|---|
| **clair** | light | **jaune** | yellow |
| **foncé** | dark | **marron** | chestnut brown |
| **blanc(he)** | white | **pourpre** | purple |
| **bleu** | blue | **rose** | pink |
| **brun** | brown | **rouge** | red |
| **gris** | gray | **vert** | green |

## *the way it works*

### *More useful verbs*

We have already seen **trouver** (to find) and looked at its pattern of endings (p. 10). There are many French verbs with this pattern and they are often referred to as **-er** verbs, because of the ending of the infinitive. There are two other main categories of French verbs: **-ir** and **-re**. Here is an example of each pattern:
**choisir** *to choose*

| | | | |
|---|---|---|---|
| je chois**is** | I choose | nous chois**issons** | we choose |
| tu chois**is** | you choose | vous chois**issez** | you choose |
| il/elle chois**it** | he/she chooses | ils/elles chois**issent** | they choose |

**vendre** *to sell*

| je vend**s** | I sell | nous vend**ons** | we sell |
| tu vend**s** | you sell | vous vend**ez** | you sell |
| il/elle vend | he/she/sells | ils/elles vend**ent** | they sell |

However, there are many verbs which do not exactly follow these patterns. Here are two such irregular verbs:

**partir** *to leave, go*

| Je par**s** | I leave | nous part**ons** | we leave |
| tu par**s** | you leave | vous part**ez** | you leave |
| il/elle part | he/she/it leaves | ils/elles part**ent** | they leave |

**prendre** *to take, have*

| je prend**s** | I take | nous pren**ons** | we take |
| tu prend**s** | you take | vous pren**ez** | you take |
| il/elle prend | he/she/it takes | ils/elles pren**nent** | they take |

### *How to say It or Them, etc. (object pronouns)*

When you are talking about something that is the *object* of the sentence, use **me, te, le, la, les** instead of **je, tu, il, elle, ils, elles**, e.g.:
Je prends le gilet: Je **le** prends—I'll take *it*.
Je prends la jupe: Je **la** prends
Je préfère les pullovers: je **les** préfère—I prefer *them*.

Before a verb beginning with a vowel, use **l'** instead of **le** or **la**:
J'aime la jupe: je **l'**aime—I like *it*.

In a negative sentence, you say: Je **ne le** prends **pas**—I won't take it.

When used as object pronouns, **nous** and **vous** remain the same.

## things to do

1 Whether you want luxury goods, camping and sports equipment, or anything else, you need to know where to buy them. Do you know where the following items can be bought? Match the item to the shop.

| 1 | une pile (battery) | **(a)** | le magasin de pêche |
| 2 | un dictionnaire (dictionary) | **(b)** | le magasin de camping |
| 3 | un filet de pêche (fishing net) | **(c)** | la librairie |
| 4 | une bouteille de parfum Dior | **(d)** | le bureau de tabac |
| 5 | des cigarettes | **(e)** | la parfumerie |
| 6 | un bracelet | **(f)** | la quincaillerie |
| 7 | un tournevis (screwdriver) | **(g)** | la droguerie |
| 8 | une poêle (frying pan) | **(h)** | la bijouterie |

Now practice asking for these items: e.g.,
Bonjour, monsieur, je voudrais une pile, s'il vous plaît. Ça fait combien?

2 You have seen a jacket that you like and you are trying it on. But somehow it isn't quite right . . .
Vendeur: Vous aimez ce blouson, monsieur?
You: [Say you don't like the color. Ask if he can show you another color, perhaps gray or brown.]

31

| Vendeur: | Oui, monsieur. Attendez, s'il vous-plaît. |
| You: | [Say this jacket is too big and ask if they have anything smaller.] |
| Vendeur: | Attendez, je vais voir. . . Oui, en voici un. Vous voulez l'essayer? |
| You: | [Yes, please.] . . .[Say it suits you and ask how much it is.] |
| Vendeur: | C'est 1000 francs. |
| You: | [Say you'll take it.] |

**3.3** After trying on some clothes you are disappointed to find that none of them fit you. Can you tell the sales clerk what's wrong?

| Vendeuse: | Vous aimez cette jupe? (too small) |
| You: | Non, elle est trop . . . |

| Vendeuse: | Vous aimez cette robe? |
| You: | . . . . . . . . . . . . . . . . . |

| Vendeuse: | Vous aimez ce pantalon? |
| You: | . . . . . . . . . . . . . . . . . |

| Vendeuse: | Vous aimez ce jean? |
| You: | . . . . . . . . . . . . . . . . . |

| Vendeuse: | Vous aimez ces chaussures? |
| You: | . . . . . . . . . . . . . . . . . |

**3.4** Can you match the two halves of these statements?

1 Ces chaussures son très confortables.
2 Cette cravate en soie fait très chic.
3 Vous préférez ces gants, madame?
4 Moi, je préfère ce chapeau noir.
5 Ce manteau est beau.

(a) Moi aussi, alors je le prends.

(b) Oui, je les préfère.

(c) Je peux l'essayer?

(d) Je la prends.

(e) Elles me plaisent.

# SHOPPING FOR FOOD

## au supermarché/at the supermarket

Agathe sends Julien and Claire to the store to buy food for the picnic.

Julien:   Qu'est-ce qu'il nous faut? (looks at the shopping list) . . . Bon,
Claire, prends un chariot.

They go around the store putting goods in the shopping cart. At the
*Viandes froides* counter they ask the attendant to help them.

Julien:   **Donnez-moi** deux grandes tranches de pâté de campagne, s'il
vous plaît. **Je voudrais aussi deux cent cinquante grammes
de** jambon . . . et **cinq cents grammes de** saucisson. Merci.

Claire:   (looking in the cart) Bon, nous avons le pâté, le jambon et le
saucisson, le fromage, **une plaquette de** beurre, **une boîte de**
thon, **une douzaine d'**œufs . . .

Julien:   Où sont les fruits? Ah, les voici.

Claire:   Regarde ces belles pêches! Et j'adore les cerises . . . Achetons
**un kilo de** ces jolies cerises, Julien. C'est parfait pour un picnic.

Julien:   D'accord. Vraiment Claire, tu es très gourmande aujourd'hui.

## USEFUL PHRASES

| | |
|---|---|
| Qu'est-ce qu'il nous faut? | What do we need? |
| Prends un chariot. | Take a shopping cart. |
| C'est parfait pour un picnic. | It's perfect for a picnic. |
| tu es très gourmande | you are very greedy |

### At the supermarket

| | |
|---|---|
| Donnez-moi . . . | Give me . . . |
| deux grandes tranches de . . . | two big slices of . . . |
| pâté de campagne | coarse paté |
| Je voudrais aussi . . . | I also want . . . |
| cinq cents grammes (un demi-kilo) de . . . | 500 grams (half a kilo) of . . . |
| deux cent cinquante grammes de . . . | 250 grams of . . . |
| cent grammes de . . . | 100 grams of . . . |
| un morceau de . . . | a piece of . . . |
| une plaquette de beurre | a slab of butter |
| une boîte de thon | a can of tuna |
| une douzaine d'œufs | a dozen eggs |
| Où sont les fruits? | Where is the fruit? |
| Regarde ces belles pêches! | Look at those lovely peaches! |
| J'adore les cerises. | I love cherries. |
| Achetons . . . | Let's buy . . . |
| un kilo de . . . | a kilo of . . . |

Le pâté – paté
Le fromage – cheese
Le beurre – butter
Le saucisson – sausage
Le thon – tuna
Les oeufs – eggs
Le jambon – ham

## Names of some common food stores

| | | | |
|---|---|---|---|
| l'alimentation | food store | le marchand de légumes | produce store |
| le supermarché | supermarket | | |
| la boulangerie | bakery | le marché | market |
| la pâtisserie | pastry shop | la crémerie | dairy |
| la confiserie | candy store | la poissonnerie | fish market |
| la boucherie | butcher shop | libre service | self-service |
| la charcuterie | delicatessen | entrée libre | no obligation to buy |
| l'épicerie | grocery store | | |

## Health foods

| | | | |
|---|---|---|---|
| alimentation naturelle | health foods | le germe du blé | wheat germ |
| les produits naturels | natural products | de culture biologique | organically grown |
| la farine intégrale | whole wheat flour | à base de plantes | plant-based |

# EATING OUT

**Restaurants**   There are many different categories of restaurants, ranging from those with several stars or forks offering a **menu gastronomique** to the modest **Routier**, which can serve some very good, simple food.

Before going into a restaurant, check the menus and prices that are displayed outside. Most offer one or more set menus which are often a good value. Look out for **le plat du jour** (today's special), and scan the set menu (**le menu**). There is usually a cover charge for each person (**le couvert**). Service of some 15% is often included in the bill (**service compris**), in which case it is up to you to choose whether to leave anything extra for a particularly good meal.

## au restaurant/at the restaurant

Bernard, Martine, Patrick, and Sylvie arrive at the Restaurant du Gourmet.

```
    MENU DU JOUR -- 90francs

       Moules marinière

      Sardines grillées

      Bisque de homard

     Escargots à l'ail

       Assiette froide
              ✐
    Saumon à l'américaine

    Raie au beurre noir
              ✐
       Selle d'agneau

      Entrecôte grillée

     Côte de porc rôti

  Salade verte ou choix de légumes
              ✐
        Glaces maison

      Fruits au saison

     Plateau de fromage
```

Martine:   **Vous avez une table pour quartre personnes?**
Garçon:    Oui, messieurs-dames. Par ici, s'il vous plaît.
(They sit down at a table)

| | |
|---|---|
| Garçon: | Voici la carte et la carte des vins. Je vous recommande le caneton aux pruneaux qui est notre spécialité d'aujourd'hui. |
| Bernard: | **On va prendre le menu du jour**. Qu'est-ce que tu prends, Sylvie? |
| Sylvie: | **Je prends les escargots, et après la selle d'agneau.** |
| Martine: | Je n'ai pas grand'faim aujourd'hui. **Apportez-moi du saumon, s'il vous plaît.** |
| Patrick: | **Et pour moi** des moules et du caneton. |
| Bernard: | **Donnez-mois** des sardines et une entrecôte, s'il vous plaît. |
| Garçon: | Oui, monsieur. Bleu, saignant, à point? |
| Bernard: | Saignant. |
| Garçon: | Très bien, monsieur, et comme boisson? |
| Bernard: | **Une bouteille de vin rouge** et une bouteille de vin blanc de la maison, s'il vous plaît. |

### Eating out

*What the waiter might say*

| | |
|---|---|
| **Vous êtes combien de personnes?** | How many are you? |
| **Par ici, s'il vous plaît.** | This way, please. |
| **Voici la carte et la carte des vins.** | Here is the menu and the wine list. |
| **Je vous recommande . . .** | I recommend . . . |
| **notre spécialité d'aujourd'hui** | our speciality today |
| **Et comme boisson?** | What will you have to drink? |
| **Le service est (non) compris.** | Service is (is not) included. |

*What you might want to say*

| | |
|---|---|
| **Pouvez-vous me recommander un bon restaurant?** | Can you recommend a good restaurant? |
| **Vous avez une table . . .?** | Do you have a table . . .? |
| **pour quatre personnes** | for four people |
| **Puis-je avoir la carte?** | Could I have the menu? |
| **le menu à prix fixe/touristique** | fixed-price menu/tourist menu |
| **la carte, la carte des vins** | the menu, the wine list |
| **On va prendre le menu du jour/le menu à 90 francs.** | We'll have the set meal of the day/ the 90-franc meal. |
| **Qu'est-ce que tu prends?** | What would you like? |
| **Je prends les escargots.** | I'll have the snails. |
| **et après la selle d'agneau** | and then the saddle of lamb |
| **Je n'ai pas grand'faim.** | I'm not very hungry. |
| **Apportez-mois du saumon.** | Bring me some salmon. |
| **Et pour moi des moules et du caneton.** | And for me the mussels and duck. |

| | |
|---|---|
| Donnez-moi des sardines et une entrecôte. | Give me some sardines and a steak. |
| bleu/saignant/à point/bien cuit | very rare/rare/medium/well done (steak) |
| Une bouteille de vin rouge/vin blanc | a bottle of red/white wine |
| de la maison | of the house |
| une carafe d'eau | a pitcher of water |
| Apportez-nous . . . | Bring us . . . |
| Donnez-moi . . . | Give me . . . |
| en supplément/en sus | extra |
| L'addition, s'il vous plaît. | The bill, please. |
| Où sont les toilettes? | Where are the toilets? |

*Puis-je avoir un couteau?* (*Could I have a knife?*)

## the way it works

### On va prendre le menu du jour

The word **on** is used a great deal in French and can mean ''one,'' ''you,'' ''we,'' ''they,'' ''people,'' etc.

| | |
|---|---|
| **On** dit que . . . | They (people) say that . . . |
| Est-ce-qu'**on** peut stationner ici? | Can one (we) park here? |
| Qu'est-ce qu'**on** mange? | What shall we eat? |

### Telling someone what to do

When you are telling or ordering someone to do something, or merely making a suggestion, you use a form of the verb called the imperative. It works like this:

| | |
|---|---|
| regard**e** ces pêches | look at these peaches (to a child, or someone you know well) |
| regard**ez** la liste | look at the list (to someone you don't know very well or more than one person) |
| regard**ons** l'horaire | let's look at the schedule |

There are many examples of verbs in the imperative in this book. Here are just a few of them:

N'oubli**ez** pas (don't forget)   attend**ez** (wait)   pren**ez** (take)   pren**ons** (let's take)

## *things to do*

**Vous faites des courses!** You are going shopping!
Here are some useful phrases when buying food.

*Weights and measures*

| | |
|---|---|
| **un kilo de** | a kilo of |
| **un demi-kilo de** | half a kilo of |
| **une livre de** | a pound of |
| **cent grammes de** | 100 grams of |
| **un litre de** | a liter of |
| **un demi-litre de** | half a liter of |

*Useful adjectives*

| | |
|---|---|
| **râpé/moulu** | grated/ground |
| **en poudre** | granulated |

*Containers and quantities*

| | |
|---|---|
| **une boîte de** | a can/a box of |
| **un paquet de** | a pack of |
| **une barquette de** | a carton of |
| **un morceau de** | a piece of |
| **une tranche de** | a slice of |
| **une plaquette de** | a slab of (butter) |
| **une douzaine de** | a dozen |
| **un peu (de)** | a little (of) |
| **beaucoup (de)** | a lot (of) |

Here is your shopping-list.

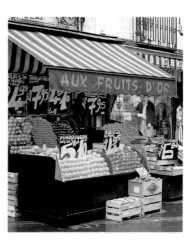

```
○ ○ ○ ○ ○ ○ ○ ○ ○ ○ ○ ○ ○ ○ ○ ○ ○ ○ ○ ○ ○ ○ ○ ○
250 grammes de beurre
1 morceau de fromage
½ kilo de sucre en poudre
1 litre de lait
200 grammes de pâté de campagne
4 tranches de jambon
1 boîte de soupe de poisson
1 kilo de pommes
1 livre de poires
½ litre de vinaigre
100 grammes de salade russe
1 barquette de carottes râpées
1 paquet de café moulu
2 bouteilles de vin rouge
1 douzaine d'oeufs
```

Practice asking for each item in turn, e.g., Je voudrais deux cent cinquante grammes de beurre.

Now say what the list would be in English.

You are in a bakery (see p. 82).

Ask for the items shown.
Ask how much it all comes to.

**3.7** You are at a restaurant with a party of friends. Tell the waiter in French what everyone would like to eat or drink.

**3.8** You could go to a café where the following conversation might take place:

Garçon: Bonjour, vous désirez?

You: **Je prends un sandwich au fromage**, s'il vous plaît.

Garçon: Très bien, et comme boisson?

You: **Un verre de cola.**

Garçon: Voilà, monsieur/mademoiselle.

You: **Merci. L'addition, s'il vous plaît.**

Here is a list of the kinds of food and drink you might want:

| | | | |
|---|---|---|---|
| un casse-croûte | snack | une omelette au fromage | cheese omelette |
| un sandwich au jambon | ham sandwich | des frites | french fries |
| un américain | ham salad sandwich | une gaufre | waffle |
| | | un hamburger | hamburger |
| un sandwich au fromage | cheese sandwich | un hot dog | hot dog |
| un croque-monsieur | grilled cheese and ham sandwich | des brochettes | kebabs |
| | | une glace | ice cream |
| | | une crêpe | pancake |

And you might like one of the following to drink:

| | | | |
|---|---|---|---|
| une jus de tomates | tomato juice | un verre de cidre | cider |
| un jus de pommes | apple juice | une (bière) blonde | lager |
| un citron pressé | lemonade | une pression | draft beer |
| une limonade | soda | un panaché | beer mixed with soda |
| un thé au lait/ nature/au citron | tea with milk/plain/ with lemon | un café noir/ crème | black coffee/coffee with milk |
| | | une express | espresso |
| un chocolat chaud | hot chocolate | un lait frappé | milk shake |
| un cola | cola | | |

Now try to make up conversations of your own!

# BANK, POST OFFICE, TELEPHONE

**Banks and paying**   Banks are open from approximately 9 to 12 and 2 to 4, except in larger towns, where they may not close for lunch. They are closed either all day Monday, or on Saturday afternoons. Banks close early the day before public holidays in France. **Bureaux de change** (currency exchange offices) are open longer hours, though rates of exchange may alter outside normal banking hours.

Credit cards are now widely accepted in shops, hotels, restaurants and many gas stations. Traveler's checks are also accepted in some hotels, shops, etc., though you will normally get a better rate of exchange from a bank.

## à la banque/at the bank

Claire and Julien want to hire a windsurfer (**une planche à voile**), but first Claire needs to go to the bank to change some checks.

Employé:   Bonjour, mademoiselle.
Claire:   Bonjour, monsieur. **Puis-je changer de l'argent?**
Employé:   Oui, mademoiselle. Vous avez des chèques de voyage?
Claire:   Oui, **Je veux encaisser ces deux chèques** de dix livres.
Employé:   Alors, signez ici, et donnez-moi votre passeport. Vingt livres, ça fait . . . (fills in form and calculates amount) Alors, voilà votre passeport, et maintenant, passez à la caisse.
Julien:   Montre-moi ton passeport, Claire. Oh, quelle jolie photo!
Claire:   Ne sois pas idiot—la photo est affreuse!
(They go to the cashier.)
Caissier:   Voilà, mademoiselle. Un billet de cent francs, deux billets de cinquante, et deux pièces de dix francs.
Julien:   Très bien. (to Claire) Allons à la plage.

### At the bank/at the currency exchange (au bureau de change)

| | |
|---|---|
| Je veux/voudrais . . . | I would like to . . . |
| Puis-je/Est-ce que je peux . . .? | Can I . . .? |
| changer de l'argent | change some money |
| changer vingt dollars | change twenty dollars |
| encaisser ces chèques de voyage/ | change these traveler's checks |
| ces chèques travellers | |
| J'ai une carte bancaire. | I have a bank card. |
| une carte de crédit | a credit card |
| un carnet de chèques | a checkbook |
| une lettre de crédit | a letter of credit |
| Quel est le taux de change aujourd'hui? | What is the exchange rate today? |
| Voici un billet de cent francs. | Here is a hundred-franc bill. |
| une pièce de dix francs | a ten-franc coin |
| cinquante centimes | fifty centimes |
| de la monnaie | some change |
| Voulez-vous remplir cette fiche/formulaire? | Would you fill out this form? |
| Signez ici. | Sign here. |
| Ça fait . . . | That comes to . . . |
| Passez à la caisse. | Go to the cashier. |

### USEFUL WORDS AND PHRASES

| | |
|---|---|
| **Montre-moi ton passeport.** | Show me your passport. |
| **Quelle jolie photo!** | What a lovely photo! |
| **Ne sois pas idiot.** | Don't be stupid. |
| **Elle est affreuse.** | It's awful. |

**Post offices and stamps** The post office (**Postes et Télécommunications —P&T/PTT**) is open from 8 a.m. to 7 p.m. Monday through Friday and from 8 a.m. to noon on Saturdays. Mailboxes in France and Switzerland are yellow, and have different slots for local and out-of-town mail. In Belgium, mailboxes are red. You can arrange to receive letters from the *Poste Restante* (general delivery) counter at central post offices, and these can be picked up for a small fee and upon production of your passport.

In France, stamps can be bought at a **bureau de tabac** (recognizable by its distinctive red cone sign), from some cafés, or from the post office.

## au bureau de tabac/at the tobacconist's

Patrick and Bernard go to a *tabac* to buy some stamps and stop to look at the postcard stand outside.

Patrick:   Il me faut cinq cartes postales. Ah, cette vue de la Seine est assez belle. Mais, qu'est-ce que c'est, Bernard?

Bernard:   Ça, c'est le Centre Georges Pompidou.

Patrick:   Ah bon? Je prends celle-là aussi. (He goes to the counter.) **Vous avez des timbres**, monsieur?

Marchand:   C'est pour quelle destination, monsieur?

Patrick:   **C'est pour l'Angleterre**—et **je veux aussi un timbre pour** les Etats-Unis.

Marchand:   J'ai des timbres pour la Grande Bretagne, mais je n'ai pas de timbres pour les Etats-Unis. Il faut aller à la poste, à côté.

Patrick:   Alors, **donnez-moi quatre timbres pour des cartes postales et un pour une lettre**, pour l'Angleterre. **Est-ce que vous vendez des journaux aussi?**

Marchand:   Non, monsieur. Le kiosque à journaux est en face.

(At the newsstand)

Marchand:   Un journal irlandais? Je regrette, monsieur, je n'ai pas de journaux irlandais—mais j'ai un journal anglais. Le voici.

Patrick:   *The Independent?* Bon, je le prends.

### At the tabac/at the post office

| | |
|---|---|
| Il me faut cinq carte postales. | I need five postcards. |
| Vous avez des timbres/un carnet de timbres? | Do you have any stamps?/a book of stamps? |
| C'est pour quelle destination? | Where is it for? |
| C'est pour l'Angleterre/la Grande Bretagne/les Etats-Unis. | It's for England/Great Britain/the USA. |
| Donnez-moi un timbre pour une lettre/pour une carte postale. | Give me a stamp for a letter/for a postcard. |
| La poste/le bureau de poste est à côté. | The post office is next door. |
| Je voudrais envoyer cette lettre/ce paquet/ce colis. | I would like to send this letter/this packet/this parcel. |
| . . . par avion/express/en recommande/ avec accusé de réception | . . . by airmail/express/registered/with recorded delivery |
| Où est la boîte aux lettres? | Where is the mailbox? |
| Où se trouve le guichet de poste restante? | Where is the general delivery counter? |
| Y a-t-il du courrier pour moi? | Is there any mail for me? |

### At the newsstand

| | |
|---|---|
| Le kiosque à journaux est en face. | The newsstand is across the street. |
| Vous avez des journaux américains? | Do you have any American newspapers? |
| Je n'ai pas de journaux irlandais. | I don't have any Irish newspapers. |
| J'ai un journal anglais. | I have an English newspaper. |

### USEFUL WORDS AND PHRASES

| | | | |
|---|---|---|---|
| Cette vue est assez belle. | That view is rather pretty. | Ça, c'est . . . | That's . . . |
| Qu'est-ce que c'est? | What's that? | Ah bon? | Really? |
| | | Je prends celle-là. | I'll take that one. |

## *Where are you from?*

### *Nationalities and languages/Les nationalités et les langues*

| | | | |
|---|---|---|---|
| **Je viens de France.** | I am from France. | **Je parle français.** | I speak French. |
| **Je suis Français(e).** | I am French. | **des journaux français** | French newspapers |

Use a capital letter when talking about someone's nationality, and a small letter when talking about the language.

**Telephones**  You can dial direct to most places. There are generally fewer public telephones than in the United States, and you can make calls from post offices (*Téléphone/Télégraphe* offices in Belgium) and hotels. Many telephones now take phone cards (**télécartes**), which can be bought at *tabacs,* etc. In France, local calls are often made from cafés (you may have to buy a **jeton**—token). Emergency numbers are Police 17, Fire 18, Operator 13.

## conversation téléphonique/telephone conversation

The Bergeron family is organizing a beach barbecue for Sunday. Claire wants to invite Cathy, an English friend who is staying with a family in a nearby town. At the camp office, she dials the number.

| | |
|---|---|
| Mme Leverd: | **Allô? Ici le 84-58-29.** |
| Claire: | **Allô, je voudrais parler à** Cathy, s'il vous plaît. |
| Mme Leverd: | Oui. C'est de la part de qui? |
| Claire: | **C'est** Claire Rogers, une camarade anglaise. |

| | |
|---|---|
| Mme Leverd: | Attendez un instant. Je vais la chercher, mais je crois qu'elle est à la poste. (Shouts, ''Cathy!''. . . Pause . . .) Non, elle n'est pas là en ce moment. Vous voulez lui laisser un message? |
| Claire: | Je voudrais l'inviter à un barbecue sur la plage à S. Jean-sur-Mer. C'est pour dimanche soir à dix-huit heures. |
| Mme Leverd: | Ah, vous êtes bien gentille. Je crois qu'elle est libre dimanche soir. |
| Claire: | **Pouvez-vous lui dire de me téléphoner** au camping? **C'est le numéro** 86-22-51. |
| Mme Leverd: | D'accord. Je vais le lui dire. Merci beaucoup, mademoiselle. Au revoir. |
| Claire: | Au revoir, madame. |

### *Using the telephone*

| | |
|---|---|
| **Allô, ici le 84-58-29.** | Hello, this is 84-58-29. |
| **Quel est votre numéro de téléphone?** | What is your telephone number? |
| **C'est bien le 84-58-29?** | Is this 84-58-29? |
| **Vous avez fait un mauvais numéro.** | |
| **Vous vous êtes trompé de numéro.** | You've got the wrong number. |
| **Vous faites erreur.** | |
| **Je voudrais parler à . . .** | I'd like to speak to . . . |
| **Vous pouvez me passer le poste 18?** | Give me extension 18. |
| **C'est de la part de qui?** | Who's speaking? |
| **Qui est à l'appareil?** | Who is it? |
| **Attendez un instant.** | Wait a moment. |
| **Je vais le/la chercher.** | I'll go and look for him/her. |
| **C'est lui-/elle-même à l'appareil.** | Yes, speaking. |
| **Ne quittez pas** (*operator*). | Hold the line, please. |

| | |
|---|---|
| Elle n'est pas là en ce moment. | She's not here at the moment. |
| Vous voulez lui laisser un message? | Do you want to leave her a message? |
| Pouvez-vous lui dire de me téléphoner? | Could you ask he to phone me? |
| Je vais le lui dire. | I'll tell her. |
| Vous voulez rappeler plus tard? | Do you want to call back later? |
| Vous pouvez répéter, s'il vous plaît? | Could you repeat that, please? |
| la cabine téléphonique | phone booth |
| téléphoner par l'automatique | to dial direct |
| composer le numéro | to dial the number |
| attendre la tonalité | to wait for the dial tone |
| une communication personelle | personal call |
| en PVC | collect call |
| le/la standardiste | operator |
| l'annuaire | directory |
| un jeton | token |
| des pièces de 5F, 1F, ½ F | 5-franc/1 franc/½ franc coins |
| l'indicatif du département | area code |

## USEFUL WORDS AND PHRASES

| | | | |
|---|---|---|---|
| la camarade | friend | Je crois que . . . | I think that . . . |
| gentil(le) | nice, kind | elle est libre | she's free |

## the way it works

### Who? and What?

Who? is **Qui est-ce qui?** or **Qui?**:

| | |
|---|---|
| **Qui est-ce qui** parle anglais? | Who speaks English? |
| **Qui** est à l'appareil? | Who is speaking? (on telephone) |

What? is **Qu'est-ce que?** or **Que?**:

| | |
|---|---|
| **Qu'est-ce que** vous faites? | What are you doing? |
| **Que** cherchez-vous? | What are you looking for? |

If you want to know what something is you use **Qu'est-ce que c'est?**:

| | |
|---|---|
| **Qu'est-ce que c'est?** C'est la Tour Eiffel. | What is it? It's the Eiffel Tower. |
| **Qu'est-ce que c'est?** C'est un hélicoptère. | What is it? It's a helicopter. |

### Which? and What?

To ask "which?" you use **Quel** before a masculine noun (**Quel** timbre? Which stamp?) and **Quelle** before a feminine noun (**Quelle** destination?).
Here are two more examples:

| | |
|---|---|
| **Quel** est le taux de change? | What is the exchange rate? |
| **Quelle** est la date aujourd'hui? | What is the date today? |

The words **Quel** and **Quelle** are also used in exclamations:

**Quel** beau temps!                        What beautiful weather!
**Quelle** jolie photo!                     What a lovely photo!

For words in the plural, use **Quels** and **Quelles**.

## This One and That One

You know how to say "this" or "that" (**ce** timbre—this stamp; **cette** carte postale—that post card). However, if you want to distinguish between "this one" and "that one," you can do it like this:

| *masculine* | | *feminine* | |
|---|---|---|---|
| **celui-ci** | this one | **celle-ci** | this one |
| **celui-là** | that one | **celle-là** | that one |
| **ceux-ci** | these ones | **celles-ci** | these ones |
| **ceux-là** | those ones | **celles-là** | those ones |

**Ceci** and **cela** refer to "this" or "that" in a general way. **Cela** is usually shortened to **ça**, and this is used a lot.

**Ça** fait trente francs.                  That comes to 30F
**Ça** c'est le Centre Georges Pompidou.    That's the Pompidou Center.

## All and everything

The word for "all" is **tout** (**tous** = plural) with a masculine noun and **toute** (**toutes** = plural) with a feminine noun. The word **tout** on its own means "everything."

Here are some common expressions using **tout/toute**:

| | |
|---|---|
| **tout** le monde | everybody |
| **tout** le temps | all the time |
| **toute** la famille | all the family |
| **toute** la soirée | all evening |
| **tous** les jours | every day (**toujours** = always) |
| **tous** les deux | both (masc.) |
| **toutes** les jeunes filles | all the girls |

## How to say you don't have any

**J'ai** means "I have": J'ai du fromage (*I have some cheese*); J'ai des journaux (*I have some newspapers*).

To say "I don't have" you use "**Je n'ai pas**": Je n'ai pas de fromage; Je n'ai pas de journaux.

Note that if the verb is negative you use the word **de** for "any" (not **des**).

## Expressions with *avoir*

**J'ai** is a form of the verb **avoir** (see Mardi p. 17 for the complete pattern). This verb can be used in a number of very common expressions meaning "I am," "you are," etc.

| | | | |
|---|---|---|---|
| **J'ai** faim/soif. | I am hungry/thirsty. | **J'ai** horreur de . . . | I hate . . . |
| **Tu as** chaud/froid. | You are hot/cold. | **Nous avons** peur. | We are frightened. |
| Quel âge **avez-vous**? | How old are you? | **Vous avez** raison. | You are right. |
| **Il a** vingt ans. | He is twenty. | **Ils ont** tort. | They are wrong. |

(NB If you want to say "I'm not hungry" you say: **Je n'ai pas faim**.)

## Some more verbs

You know how to say "I would like" (je **voudrais**) and "Do you want?" (**voulez-vous?**). Here is the verb **vouloir** (to wish or want):

| | |
|---|---|
| je **veux** | nous **voulons** |
| tu **veux** | vous **voulez** |
| il/elle **veut** | ils/elles **veulent** |

Two other useful verbs are **venir** (to come) and **pouvoir** (to be able):

| | | | |
|---|---|---|---|
| Je **viens** | nous **venons** | je **peux** (I can) | nous **pouvons** |
| tu **viens** | vous **venez** | tu **peux** | vous **pouvez** |
| il/elle **vient** | ils/elles **viennent** | il/elle **peut** | ils/elles **peuvent** |

## Pronouns—the indirect object

Sometimes a sentence has what is called an "indirect object." Look at this sentence from the third dialogue:

Vous voulez lui laisser un message?  Do you want to leave her a message?

In this sentence, the message is the direct object and Cathy ("her") is the indirect object.

In French, the pronouns **me, te, nous** and **vous** are used for both direct and indirect objects, but **lui** and **leur** are used for indirect objects only.
Look for the indirect object after these verbs:

| | | |
|---|---|---|
| parler (to speak): | Je parle à ma mère. | Je **lui** parle. (I speak to her.) |
| téléphoner (to phone): | Elle téléphone à ses amies. | Elle **leur** téléphone. (She phones them.) |
| dire (to say): | Je dis à cet enfant . . . | Je **lui** dis . . . (I say to him . . .) |
| donner (to give): | Je donne à ces garçons . . . | Je **leur** donne . . . (I give them . . .) |
| écrire (to write): | Vous écrivez à votre père. | Vous **lui** écrivez. (You write to him.) |

You would also say:

| | |
|---|---|
| Il **me** parle. (He speaks to me.) | Je **te** donne. (I give (to) you.) |
| Elle **nous** écrit. (She writes to us.) | Ils **vous** téléphonent. (They telephone you.) |

## Reflexive verbs

You may have noticed in this book some verbs which have, for example, **me, te** or **se** placed between the subject and the verb itself: je **m**'appelle, je **me** présente, etc. These are called reflexive pronouns and they can often be translated by using the words "myself," "yourself," etc.

appeler to call   **s'**appeler to be called (call oneself)

Here is the full list of reflexive pronouns:

| | | | | |
|---|---|---|---|---|
| **me** | myself | | **nous** | ourselves |
| **te** | yourself | | **vous** | yourselves |
| **se** | himself/herself/oneself | | **se** | themselves |

## *things to do*

**.1** Can you match up these pairs of sentences so that they make sense?

1 Regardez les Alpes!
2 Est-ce que vous avez des journaux?
3 Ah Bernard, c'est vous?
4 Je voudrais envoyer cette lettre.
5 Vous voulez encaisser ces chèques?
6 Je voudrais des cigarettes, s'il vous plaît.

(a) C'est pour quelle destination?
(b) Quelle jolie vue!
(c) Quels journaux voulez-vous?
(d) Quelle marque (brand) voulez-vous?
(e) Quelle surprise!
(f) Quel est le taux de change?

**.2** Say what you want
In the supermarket you need various items at the delicatessen counter and it's a matter of pointing out to the attendant which cheese, etc., you want. Use **celui-ci** or **celui-là**, **celle-ci** or **celle-là** in your answer.

Assistant: Quel fromage voulez-vous, madame? Celui-ci ou celui-là?
You: [This one please.]
Assistant: Et quelle quiche voulez-vous, madame?
You: [That one, please.]
Assistant: Et quel pâté voulez-vous, madame?
You: [This one, please.]
Assistant: Quel saucisson voulez-vous, madame?
You: [This one and that one, please.] Je prends du fromage, de la quiche, du pâté et des saucissons.

**.3** You are at a post office in France. Tell the clerk what you need:
Assistant: Bonjour, monsieur/madame. Vous désirez?
Vous: [Tell him you want to buy some stamps.]
Assistant: Pour des lettres ou pour des cartes postales?
Vous: [Say you want to send one letter and two postcards.]
Assistant: Très bien. C'est pour quelle destination?
Vous: [Tell him the letter is for England, and the postcards are for the USA.]
Assistant: C'est tout?
Vous: [Say no, you want to send a package to Paris.]

**4.4** You are in a bank.
1 Ask the teller what the day's exchange rate is.
2 Ask whether you can cash a check.
3 Say you want to exchange $50 worth of traveler's checks.
4 Say you want to exchange a 100-franc bill for ten 10-franc coins.

**4.5** See if you can complete this telephone conversation. Look in the phrasebook section if you get stuck.

Vous: ................................................................

Mme Gérard: Oui, c'est le 87-23-25.

Vous: ................................................................

Mme Gérard: Vous voulez parlez à M. Lotte? C'est de la part de qui?

Vous: ................................................................

Mme Gérard: Oh pardon—il n'est pas là en ce moment.

Vous: [Ask if he can call you back.] .........................

Mme Gérard: Quel est votre numéro?

Vous: ................................................................

Mme Gérard: Bon, je vais lui donner le message. Merci et au revoir.

Vous: ................................................................

**4.6** See if you can shorten these sentences by using indirect object pronouns. The first one is done for you.
1 Claire parle à l'employé de banque.
Claire lui parle.
2 Bernard dit bonjour à la marchande de tabac.
Bernard ................................................................
3 Le caissier donne un billet de 100F à Julien.
Le caissier ................................................................
4 Agathe téléphone à son mari.
Elle ................................................................
5 Claire écrit à ses parents en Angleterre.
Elle ................................................................

# ILLNESS AND ACCIDENTS

**The pharmacy**    A **pharmacie** is a pharmacy, while a **droguerie** (similar to a drugstore) sells household goods and toiletries. The **pharmacie** can be recognized by its illuminated green cross in the window. You can go to the **pharmacien** for helpful medical advice as well as for first aid treatment. A schedule of local pharmacies open at night is posted in the shop.

## à la pharmacie/at the pharmacy

Bernard has eaten and drunk too much at the restaurant and is paying a visit to the pharmacist.

| | |
|---|---|
| Bernard: | **Ah, j'ai mal à la tête.** |
| Pharmacienne: | Vous avez de la fièvre? |
| Bernard: | Non, mais hier j'ai trop mangé et trop bu. **Est-ce que vous avez quelque chose contre une gueule be bois?** |

| Pharmacienne: | Voyons, monsieur, vous avez sans doute une crise de foie. Je vous recommande ces comprimés que vous devez prendre trois fois par jour. Mais il faut boire seulement de l'eau pendant trois jours—vous allez vous sentir mieux bientôt. |
| Bernard: | Ah bon? Merci, je l'espère bien. |

**Illness**  You might wish to purchase traveler's insurance before leaving for France. Check with your insurance agent. In cases of minor injuries and illnesses, you will usually find the pharmacist is very helpful. Pharmacists may sell and recommend medicine that is often only available in the U.S. by prescription. If you take prescription medicine, always carry your prescription with you.

## Un accident

Julien and Claire did not have a very successful morning's windsurfing, and Julien has hurt his leg.

| Agathe: | Ah mon Dieu, qu'est-ce qui est arrivé? |
| Julien: | (groaning) C'est ma jambe. **J'ai mal à la jambe.** |
| Claire: | Oui, il est tombé dans l'eau plusieurs fois, et il s'est fait vraiment mal à la jambe. Il est très maladroit, n'est-ce pas? |
| Agathe: | Tu es couvert de bleus, Julien. Il faut t'emmener chez le médecin! |

## In the doctor's office

| Médecin: | Alors, c'est le genou qui vous fait mal? |
| Julien: | **Non, docteur, c'est la cheville. Elle est toute gonflée.** |
| Médecin: | (examining the ankle) Ça fait mal ici? |
| Julien: | Aïe, ne touchez pas, je vous en prie. C'est très douloureux. |
| Médecin: | (tutting) A mon avis, ce n'est pas trop grave. Mais pour nous en assurer, je vais vous envoyer à l'hôpital pour passer des radios. En attendant, je vais vous panser la cheville, jeune homme. |
| Julien: | Oh non! Mes vacances sont gâchées! |

## Illnesses and injuries

| | |
|---|---|
| Je ne me sens pas bien/Ça ne va pas bien/Je ne vais pas bien. | I don't feel well. |
| Je suis malade/Je suis blessé(e). | I am ill/I am hurt. |
| J'ai mal à/au/aux . . . | My . . . hurts.* |
| J'ai mal à la tête/au ventre. | I have a headache/a stomachache. |
| au cœur. | I feel sick. |
| J'ai mal partout. | I ache everywhere. |
| J'ai vomi. | I vomited. |
| J'ai une crise de foie. | I have an upset stomach. |
| Je tousse. | I have a cough. |
| J'ai un rhume. | I have a cold. |
| J'ai attrapé un coup de soleil. | I have a sunburn. |
| J'ai mal aux dents. | I have a toothache. |
| aux gencives | sore gums |
| Etes-vous blessé(e)? | Are you hurt? |
| Je me suis foulé le poignet. | I have sprained by wrist. |
| cogné la tête | banged my head |
| brûlé la main | burned my hand |
| coupé le pied | cut my foot |
| tordu le genou* | twisted my knee |
| Il s'est fait mal à la jambe. | He has hurt his leg. |
| Il est tombé dans l'eau. | He fell in the water. |
| Tu es couvert de bleus! | You're covered with bruises! |
| Le bras est cassé. | The (my) arm is broken. |
| La cheville est gonflée. | The (my) ankle is swollen. |
| Ne touchez pas . . . c'est douloureux! | Don't touch . . . it's painful! |
| Je suis allergique à la pénicilline. | I am allergic to penicillin. |
| Je suis cadiaque. | I have a heart condition. |
| Je suis asthmatique. | I am asthmatic. |
| Je suis diabétique. | I am diabetic. |
| Je suis enceinte. | I am pregnant. |
| Je prends la pilule. | I am on the pill. |
| J'ai perdu mes comprimés. | I have lost my pills. |

*Note that where in English, you would say "*my* head," etc., in French you generally use **le**, **la** or **les** when talking about parts of the body.

## Medical advice

| | |
|---|---|
| Il faut emmener Julien chez le médicin. | We must take Julien to see the doctor. |
| Je voudrais un rendez-vous. | I'd like an appointment. |
| Vous avez l'air malade. | You look ill. |
| Vous avez de la fièvre? | Do you have a temperature? |
| C'est le genou qui vous fait mal? | Is it your knee that's hurting? |
| Ça fait mal ici? | Does this hurt? |
| Ce n'est pas trop grave. | It isn't too serious. |
| Ne vous inquiétez pas. | Don't worry. |
| Reposez-vous | Rest (yourself). |
| Vous devez en prendre soin. | Look after it. |
| Vous devez garder le lit. | You must stay in bed. |
| Je vais vous envoyer à l'hôpital pour passer des radios. | I'm going to send you to hospital to have an X ray. |

| | |
|---|---|
| Je vais vous panser la cheville. | I will bandage your ankle. |
| Il vous faut un plâtre. | You need a cast. |
| Je vais vous faire une piqûre. | I'm going to give you an injection. |
| Je vais vous faire une ordonnance. | I'm going to give you a prescription. |
| Je vous recommande . . . | I recommend . . . |
| Vous devez prendre . . . | You must take . . . |
| Prenez des calmants. | Take painkillers. |
| trois fois par jour | three times a day |
| Je vous conseille de | I advise you to |
| . . . manger très peu | . . . eat very little |
| . . . boire seulement de l'eau | . . . drink only water |
| Vous allez vous sentir mieux bientôt. | You will feel better soon. |
| le médecin | doctor |
| Les heures de consultation | Office hours |
| Le service d'urgence | Emergency room |
| | |
| J'ai trop mangé et trop bu. | I had too much to eat and drink. |
| Je voudrais quelque chose contre . . . | I want someting for . . . |
| le constipation/la diarrhée | constipation/diarrhea |
| la dyspépsie/la flatulence/la gueule de bois | indigestion/wind/a hangover |
| Je me suis fait piquer par | I have been stung by |
| une méduse/un oursin/ un moustique/une guêpe | a jellyfish/a sea urchin/ a mosquito/a wasp |
| une cuillerée à café | a spoonful |
| avant/après les repas | before/after meals |
| pendant trois jours | for three days |

## USEFUL WORDS AND PHRASES

| | | | |
|---|---|---|---|
| hier | yesterday | maladroit | clumsy |
| voyons | let's see | je vous en prie | Please |
| sans doute | no doubt | à mon avis | in my opinion |
| que | which/that | pour nous en assurer | to reassure ourselves |
| Ah bon? | Really? | en attendant | in the meantime |
| Je l'espère bien. | I hope so. | Mes vacances sont gâchées! | My vacation is ruined! |
| Qu'est-ce qui est arrivé? | What happened? | | |

## *the way it works*

### Devoir (must, ought to, have to)

To say ''you must'' do something in French you use a form of the verb **devoir** + a second verb in the infinitive:

| | |
|---|---|
| **Je dois** partir tout de suite. | I must leave at once. |
| **Vous devez** garder le lit. | You must stay in bed. |
| **Vous devez** prendre les comprimés. | You must take the pills. |

Here is the complete verb:

| | |
|---|---|
| je **dois** | nous **devons** |
| tu **dois** | vous **devez** |
| il/elle **doit** | ils/elles **doivent** |

### What happened yesterday? (Qu'est-ce qui s'est passé hier?)

If you are talking about something that happened yesterday, you will need to use a verb in the **past tense**. In this unit you will find several examples of verbs in the past tense, e.g., Bernard **ate** and **drank** too much; Julien **fell** into the water.

The simple past tense in French uses either **avoir** or **être** and a form of the verb called the past participle. Here are some examples using **avoir**:

| | |
|---|---|
| Le vendredi je mange de poisson. | On Fridays I eat fish. |
| Hier, **J'ai mangé** des moules. | Yesterday, I ate some mussels. |
| Je travaille chez moi tous les matins. | I work at home every morning. |
| La semaine dernière **j'ai travaillé** l'après-midi aussi. | Last week I worked in the afternoon too. |

Many verbs in French have past participles ending in **é**. Unfortunately, however, there are a number of different past participle endings, which must be learned. Here is a list of some common verbs and their past participles:

| | | | |
|---|---|---|---|
| attendre (to wait for) | **attendu** | être (to be) | **été** |
| avoir (to have) | **eu** | faire (to do, make) | **fait** |
| boire (to drink) | **bu** | finir (to finish) | **fini** |
| comprendre (to understand) | **compris** | lire (to read) | **lu** |
| dire (to say) | **dit** | prendre (to take) | **pris** |
| dormir (to sleep) | **dormi** | voir (to see) | **vu** |

### Qui and que (who, that, which)

When referring to the object of a sentence, use **que** instead of **qui**:

| | |
|---|---|
| Le médicament **qui** est dans la bouteille verte a un très mauvais goût. | The medicine that is in the green bottle tastes very bad. |
| Le médicament **que** Claire a acheté est meilleur. | The medicine that Claire bought is better. |

## things to do

**5.1** A hypochondriac is arriving at the doctor's office. Can you tell what's wrong with him? Begin: **Il a mal . . .**(See list on p. 83.)

1    2    3

4    5    6

**5.2** At the pharmacy. (See list on p. 81)

    **1** You want to buy something to prevent sunburn. What do you ask for?
       **(a)** la crème à raser    **(b)** la crème solaire    **(c)** la pellicule

    **2** You need a bandage for your finger. Do you ask for
       **(a)** de la pommade    **(b)** du tricostéril    **(c)** du sparadrap?

    **3** The pharmacist gives you your mediation and tells you to take the pills twice a day after meals. Does he tell you
       **(a)** deux fois par jour avant les repas    **(b)** trois fois par jour après les repas    **(c)** deux fois par jour après les repas?

    **4** You go to the pharmacy to buy toothpaste, soap, and razor blades. What do you ask for?
       **(a)** du dentifrice, du savon et des lames à raser    **(b)** une brosse à dents, du savon et des lames à raser    **(c)** du dentifrice, du savon et de la crème à raser

# BUYING GAS AND DRIVING

**Driving**   An international driver's license is not necessary for driving in France if you are traveling on vacation. National car rental chains have offices in all the airports and cities, as well as in many smaller towns. Remember that in Europe, most cars have standard transmission. If you want to rent a car with automatic transmission, you must request one when you reserve in advance. It is a good idea to carry comprehensive insurance and make certain that the registration and rental contract are in the car at all times. Wearing your seatbelt is compulsory in France, and you can be pulled over for not having it on. You are not allowed to stop on an open road, unless you drive right off the road.

You must give way to the right (**priorité à droite**) in towns and cities, although elsewhere, main roads now have the right of way. You should look out for the signs: **Vous n'avez pas priorité** (You do not have right of way) and **Passage protégé** (right of way). Note that moving violations often carry on-the-spot fines.

**Freeways** have phones at intervals of 2 km and all-night gas stations every 20 km. Many freeways in France have tolls (**autoroute à péage**). In Switzerland, you need to buy a sticker for your windshield before using a freeway.

French roads are designated as follows: **autoroute (A)** (freeway); **route nationale (N)** (main road); **route départementale (D)** (secondary road); **route européenne (E)** (minor road); **route forestière (RF)** (forest road).

## à la station-service/at the gas station

The van carrying Patrick's display stands is on its way to Roissy. The driver stops to buy gas.

| | |
|---|---|
| Pompiste: | Bonjour, monsieur. |
| Conducteur: | Bonjour, madame. **Trente litres d'essence, s'il vous plaît.** |
| Pompiste: | Ordinaire ou super? |
| Conducteur: | **Super.** |
| Pompiste: | (fills tank) Voilà, monsieur, ça fait 115F. Merci et au revoir. |

▶ ▶ ▶ **On the road**   French **speed limits** are as follows: 130 kmph (80 mph) on toll roads, 110 (68) on freeways and divided highways, 90 (56) on other roads and 60 (37) in town. Note that all speed limits are reduced on wet roads. Drinking and driving carries a heavy fine, and there are random breath tests. **Parking restrictions** vary from town to town, but may be on one or other side of the street at different times of the month. Most downtown areas have parking zones, and in **zone bleue** areas, parking disks (**disques de stationnement**) must be set to the time of arrival and length of stay. These can be obtained from newsstands, tourist offices and gas stations.

## un accrochage/an accident

The driver turns out of the gas station into the road but doesn't see a Renault 5 that is approaching quite fast . . . The gas station attendant is the first on the scene.

| | |
|---|---|
| Pompiste: | (to driver of Renault 5) Vous êtes blessée, mademoiselle? |
| Conductrice: | Ah, mon bras, **Je crois qu'il est cassé.** |
| Pompiste: | (to first driver) C'est de votre faute, monsieur. |
| Conducteur: | **Je suis vraiment désolé,** mademoiselle, je ne vous ai pas vue. |
| Conductrice: | Qu'est-ce que j'ai mal, mon bras, mon bras! |
| Pompiste: | Mon fils a déjà appelé une ambulance. Ne vous inquiétez pas, mademoiselle. Venez vous asseoir, reposez-vous. |
| Conducteur: | Mon Dieu, quelle catastrophe! Je suis déjà en retard! |
| Pompiste: | Calmez-vous, monsieur. Voici la police. Tout va s'arranger. |

## A la station-service (at the gas station)

| | |
|---|---|
| 30 litres d'essence, s'il vous plaît | 30 litres of gas, please |
| 50 francs, s'il vous plaît | 50 francs' worth, please |
| Faites le plein. | Fill it up. |
| Ordinaire ou super? | 2-star or 4-star? (regular or super) |
| l'essence sans plomb | unleaded gas |
| le gasoil | diesel |
| Donnez-moi de l'huile, s.v.p. | I'd like some oil, please. |
| Donnez-moi de l'eau. | I'd like some water. |
| Je voudrais vérifier la pression des pneus. | I'd like to check the tire pressure. |

## Au garage (at the garage)

| | |
|---|---|
| Je suis en panne. | My car has broken down. |
| J'ai un pneu crevé. | I've got a flat tire. |
| Est-ce que vous avez un service de dépannage? | Do you have road service? |
| Ça ne marche pas. | It's not working. |
| L'auto ne démarre pas. | The car won't start. |

## Road signs

| | |
|---|---|
| Allumez vos phares. | Turn on your lights. |
| Attention travaux | Roadwork ahead |
| Chaussée déformée | Damaged road surface |
| Déviation | Detour |
| Interdiction de doubler | No passing |
| Passage à niveau | Railroad crossing |
| Poids lourds | Heavy loads |
| Ralentir | Slow down |
| Stationnement interdit | No parking |
| Sens interdit | No entry |
| Verglas | Icy road |
| Virages sur 2 km | Curves for 2 km |

61

### Accidents and emergencies

| | |
|---|---|
| Au secours!/Vite! | Help!/Quick! |
| Qu'est-ce qui est arrivé? | What happened? |
| Il y a eu un accident/accrochage. | There's been an accident/collision. |
| Il y a des blessés. | Some people have been hurt. |
| Il faut appeler une ambulance/la police. | We must call an ambulance/the police. |
| le commissariat/le poste de police | police station |
| Il faut l'emmener à l'hôpital. | We must take him/her to the hospital. |
| les premiers soins | first aid |
| emplacements des postes de secours | location of first aid stations |
| la sortie de secours | emergency exit |
| glace à briser | break the glass |
| en cas d'accident | in case of accident |
| le sauvetage en mer | sea rescue |
| le gilet de sauvetage | life jacket |
| les sapeurs-pompiers | fire department |
| Donnez-moi votre nom et votre adresse. | Give me your name and address. |
| . . . votre premis de conduire | . . . your driver's license |
| la police d'assurance | insurance policy |
| faire un constat | fill out an accident report form |
| la contravention | fine |
| Vous étiez en tort. | You were in the wrong. |
| C'est de votre faute. | It's your fault |
| Je voudrais signaler un vol. | I'd like to report a theft. |
| J'ai perdu/On m'a volé . . . | I've lost/Somebody's stolen . . . |
| . . . ma clé/mon argent/ | . . . my key/my money/ |
| mon portefeuille/ | my wallet/ |
| mon porte-monnaie/mon sac/ | my change purse/my bag/ |
| mon appareil-photo | my camera |
| Je suis désolé. | I'm sorry. |
| Tout va s'arranger. | It'll all get sorted out. |
| Je suis en retard. | I'm late. |

## the way it works

### More about the past tense

Here are some examples of verbs which use **être** to form the past tense:
1  Le docteur **est arrivé** de bonne heure. The doctor arrived early.
2  Julien **est tombé** dans l'eau. Julien fell in the water.
3  Claire **est allée** au bureau de poste pour téléphoner. Claire went to the post office to make a phone call.

You will notice from this last example that with verbs using **être** in the past tense, the past participle has to agree with the subject of the verb. Luckily, only a small number of verbs take **être** and those that do can be easily learned. Here is a list of most of them, together with their past participles:

| | | | |
|---|---|---|---|
| aller (to go) | allé | partir (to depart) | parti |
| arriver (to arrive) | arrivé | rester (to stay) | resté |
| descendre (to go down) | descendu | retourner (to return) | retourné |
| entrer (to enter) | entré | sortir (to go out) | sorti |
| monter (to go up) | monté | tomber (to fall) | tombé |
| mourir (to die) | mort | (re)venir (to come (back)) | (re)venu |

### Reflexive verbs in the past tense

Reflexive verbs use **être** in the past tense:

| | |
|---|---|
| Julien **s'est levé** de bonne heure. | Julien got up early. |
| Claire **s'est réveillée** peu après. | Claire woke up soon afterwards. |
| Ils **se sont habillés**. | They got dressed. |

Note also ways of saying "I have hurt myself," etc.

| | |
|---|---|
| Je **me suis fait** mal. | I have hurt myself. |
| Je **me suis tordu** la jambe. | I have twisted my leg. |
| Je **me suis coupé** le doigt. | I have cut my finger. |

## things to do

**3** You are at the gas station. Tell the attendant in French:
- **(a)** to fill the tank
- **(b)** that you want 25 liters of super
- **(c)** to give you some oil
- **(d)** to give you some water for the battery
- **(e)** that you want to check the tire pressure

**4** You are at a garage. Tell the attendant:
- **(a)** you have broken down
- **(b)** your car won't start
- **(c)** your brakes are not working

Ask him if he runs a road service, and say you are in a hurry (*Je suis pressé(e)*) because you're already late.

**5** **1** You see the street sign **SENS INTERDIT**. What does it mean?
- **(a)** no parking    **(b)** no entry    **(c)** no passing

   **2** You've been involved in a collision and need to sort out some details. Can you remember the French for:
- **(a)** name and address    **(b)** driver's license    **(c)** insurance policy
- **(d)** accident report form

   **3** What does the sign **SORTIE DE SECOURS** mean?
- **(a)** first aid    **(b)** strong room    **(c)** emergency exit

## SPORTS AND LEISURE

### au centre des sports/at the sports complex

Julien and Claire arrive at the sports complex and consult the program of activities.

Claire: Voyons . . . Qu'est-ce qu'on peut faire ici? (reads) Badminton, tennis, natation, judo, danse, tir à l'arc, mini-golf—ah, j'adore ça. **Tu aimes le mini-golf?**

Julien: **Non, pas du tout. Je joue au badminton** et au tennis, mais pas aujourd'hui à cause de ma jambe. **J'aime bien nager** mais le judo—je n'en sais rien . . . (He sees another notice) Aha, regarde, Claire, tu vois **il y a un match de football** au grand stade cet après-midi. **J'ai envie d'y aller.**

Claire: **Ça ne m'intéresse pas** du tout. Toi, **tu vas assister au match** et moi **je vais jouer au golf**, d'accord?

Julien: OK. (Looks at his watch) Le match commence à deux heures. Je vais te quitter maintenant. On se rencontrera ici à quatre heures et demie.

Claire: Bon, d'accord. A tout à l'heure.

### At the sports center

| | |
|---|---|
| Qu'est-ce qu'on peut faire ici? | What can one do here? |
| la natation, la danse, le tir à l'arc | swimming, dancing, archery |
| Tu aimes le mini-golf? | Do you like miniature golf? |
| Pas du tout. | Not at all. |
| Je joue au badminton/au tennis. | I play badminton/tennis. |
| pas aujourd'hui | not today |
| à cause de ma jambe | because of my leg |
| J'aime bien nager. | I like swimming very much. |
| Je n'en sais rien. | I don't know anything about it. |
| Il y a un match de football. | There is a soccer game. |
| J'ai envie d'y aller. | I would like to go. |
| Ça ne m'intéresse pas. | That doesn't interest me. |
| Tu vas assister au match. | You go and watch the game. |
| Je vais jouer au mini-golf. | I'm going to play miniature golf. |
| Je vais te quitter maintenant. | I'll leave you now. |
| On se rencontrera ici. | We'll meet here. |
| A tout à l'heure. | See you later. |

### Sports and games

Je vais jouer . . . I'm going to play . . .
J'aime faire du/de la . . . I enjoy . . .
Je voudrais louer une raquette.
   I'd like to rent a racket.
Je voudrais un abonnement/
   un permis pour une semaine.
   I'd like a season ticket/
   permit for one week.
Je voudrais prendre des leçons.
   I'd like to take some lessons.

l'après-midi

# SIGHTSEEING

**Museums**   You normally pay an entrance fee for national museums, with a 50% discount on Sundays. Children, students and senior citizens pay less. Some museums are free on Wednesdays or Sundays. All museums are closed at Easter (**Pâcques**), Christmas (**Noël**), and other public holidays (**Jours Fériés**), and most close on Tuesdays.

There are many national and local festivals. The tourist office (**Syndicat d'Initiative**) will be able to give you details of these and any other local events, exhibitions, concerts, etc.

## un après-midi libre/an afternoon off

Bernard and Martine are planning how to spend their afternoon.

| | |
|---|---|
| Bernard: | **Qu'est-ce que tu voudrais faire** cet après-midi, chérie? |
| Martine: | **J'aimerais bien aller au Centre Pompidou.** Je n'y suis jamais allée. |
| Bernard: | Au Centre Pompidou—**c'est une bonne idée.** Ils ont toujours de belles expositions de photographie là-bas. |
| Martine: | **Moi je préfère les expositions d'art moderne.** |
| Bernard: | Il y a quelque chose pour tous les goûts au Centre Pompidou. Et ce soir **on pourra peut-être aller à un concert.** |
| Martine: | **Oui, ça me plairait beaucoup.** |
| (At the Pompidou Center) | |
| Martine: | Aha Renseignements . . . (reading aloud) Regarde—samedi le vingt et un mars, c'est aujourd'hui, n'est-ce-pas? Il y a un concert de musique française à vingt heures trente. Les tickets sont à 40 francs. |
| Bernard: | C'est de la musique classique, crois-tu? |
| Martine: | Mais oui, bien sûr. De la bonne musique. |
| Bernard: | **J'aime mieux** trouver un autre concert—du jazz, peut-être. . . |
| Martine: | **Je déteste** le jazz. |
| Bernard: | Et moi, **J'ai horreur de** la musique classique. |
| Martine: | Allons prendre un verre à la cafétéria du cinquième étage, et discutons ça un peu. |

# ENTERTAINMENT

**Le cinéma**  Many American and British films are shown in France, either with subtitles (the more serious) or dubbed (Westerns, thrillers, etc). Look in the newspapers (**la page des spectacles**) or entertainment guides for details. Performances (which are not usually continuous) run from about 2 p.m. (**la première séance**) to a late showing at 10 p.m. It is unusual to be able to buy tickets in advance. The usher (**l'ouvreuse**) will expect a tip after showing you to your seat.

## une soirée au cinéma/an evening at the movies

Patrick and Sylvie decide to go to the movies.

Patrick:   **Tu aimerais aller au cinéma** ce soir?
Sylvie:    **Oui, avec plaisir. Quel film voudrais-tu voir?**
Patrick:   Oh, **Je ne sais pas, ça m'est égal. J'aime bien les westerns,** et toi?
Sylvie:    Moi, **je préfère les films d'aventure,** ou les films policiers—même les films de science-fiction. Consultons la page des spectacles.

(They look at the entertainment page.)

Patrick:   Voilà . . . Cinéma . . . Que penses-tu de ce film de Woody Allen?
Sylvie:    Oh non, **ça ne me dit rien.** Mais regarde! On joue un Tati à La Lumière. **J'aimerais bien voir ça.**
Patrick:   Bon, allons-y. **A quelle heure commence la première séance** du soir?
Sylvie:    **Elle commence à sept heures** et à La Lumière on peut réserver les billets d'avance.

### What would you like to do?

| | |
|---|---|
| Qu'est-ce que tu voudrais faire? | What would you like to do? |
| J'aimerais bien aller . . . | I'd like to go . . . |
| Je n'y suis jamais allée. | I've never been there. |
| C'est une bonne idée. | It's a good idea. |
| Tu aimerais aller au cinéma? | Would you like to go to the movies? |
| Quel film voudrais-tu voir? | What film would you like to see? |
| Ça m'est égal. | I don't care/It's all the same to me. |

| | |
|---|---|
| Ça te dirait d'aller au théâtre? | Would you like to go to the theater? |
| Si on allait au musée? | Shall we go to the museum? |
| On pourrait aller à un concert. | We could go to a concert. |
| J'aimerais bien voir ça. | I'd love to see that. |
| J'ai grande envie d'y aller. | I'd really like to go. |
| Oui, avec plaisir. | Yes, I'd love to. |
| Ça me plairait beaucoup. | |

## Going to an art gallery (le musée d'art) or exhibition

| | |
|---|---|
| une belle exposition de photographie | a beautiful photography exhibit |
| une exposition d'art moderne | a modern art exhibit |
| quelque chose pour tous les goûts | something for all tastes |
| la peinture | painting |
| une œuvre | work of art |
| le peintre | painter |
| le dessin | drawing |

## Going to a concert, ballet or opera

| | |
|---|---|
| la salle de concert | concert hall |
| le concert de musique classique/pop | concert of classical music/pop music |
| le concert de jazz | jazz concert |
| les chanteurs | singers |
| l'orchestre | orchestra |
| les solistes | soloists |

## Going to the movies or theater

| | |
|---|---|
| un film d'aventure/de science-fiction | an adventure/science fiction film |
| un film policier/un western | a detective film/a western |
| un dessin animé | a cartoon |
| un film doublé/avec sous-titres | a dubbed film/film with subtitles |
| V.O.—version originale | undubbed foreign film |
| V.F.—version française | foreign film which has been dubbed |
| passer un film/jouer un film | to show a film |
| A quelle heure commence . . . | What time does . . . begin? |
| le film principal | the feature film |
| la première séance | the first session |
| le spectacle? | the performance |
| Faut-il donner un pourboire à l'ouvreuse? | Should one tip the usher? |

## Asking someone's opinion

| | |
|---|---|
| Que pensez-vous du nouveau film de Spielberg? | What do you think of Spielberg's new film? |
| Comment trouves-tu le théâtre français? | How do you like the French theater? |
| Tu aimes la musique classique? | Do you like classical music? |
| Ça te plaît, les expositions de photographie? | Do you like photography exhibits? |

## Giving your opinion of something

| | |
|---|---|
| J'aime les westerns. | I like westerns. |
| J'aime bien les musées. | I like museums very much. |
| J'adore le ballet russe. | I love the Russian ballet. |
| Ça me plaît, les matchs de football. | I like soccer games. |
| Ça m'ennuie, le mini-golf. | I find miniature golf boring. |
| Je préfère le tennis. | I prefer tennis. |
| J'aime mieux les films policiers. | I prefer detective films. |
| Ça ne me dit rien. | That doesn't interest me. |
| Je n'aime pas la musique pop. | I don't like pop music. |
| Je n'aime pas du tout le rugby. | I don't like rugby at all. |
| Je déteste le jazz. | I hate jazz. |
| J'ai horreur de l'opéra. | I hate opera. |
| Discutons ça un peu. | Let's talk about it. |

## Buying tickets for concerts, theaters, museums, etc.

| | |
|---|---|
| Y a-t-il des places? | Are there any seats? |
| Peut-on acheter des billets d'avance? | Can you buy tickets in advance? |
| Je voudrais réserver des places. | I would like to reserve some seats. |
| Il reste quelques places. | There are a few seats left. |
| Combien coûtent les places au balcon? | How much are the seats in the balcony? |
| . . . au parterre/à l'orchestre? | . . . on the ground floor? |
| . . . à la seconde galerie? | . . . in the second balcony? |
| Je voudrais deux tickets de 40 francs. | I'd like two tickets for 40 francs. |
| Des retours de dernière minute. | Last-minute returns. |
| Combien coûtent les billets? | How much are the tickets? |
| Y a-t-il des réductions pour . . . ? | Are there any discounts for . . .? |
| . . . les enfants/les étudiants? | . . . children/students? |
| . . . les retraités/les chômeurs? | . . . retired people/unemployed people? |
| Avez-vous un guide? | Do you have a guidebook? |
| entrée libre | entrance free |

## Opening times (Heures d'ouverture)

| | |
|---|---|
| Ouvert . . . /Fermé . . . | Open . . . /Closed . . . |
| A quelle heure est-ce que ça ouvre? | What time does it open? |
| A quelle heure est-ce que ça ferme? | What time does it close? |
| Est-ce que le musée est ouvert le mardi? | Is the museum open on Tuesdays? |

## Dates

| | |
|---|---|
| Quelle est la date aujourd'hui? | What is the date today? |
| C'est . . . | It's . . . |
| samedi le vingt et un mars | Saturday, March 21st |
| le premier avril | April 1st |
| le deux juin | June 2nd |
| le onze novembre | November 11th (Veteran's Day) |
| le quatorze juillet | July 14th (Bastille Day) |
| le vingt-cinq décembre | December 25th |
| mille neuf cent quatre-vingt-douze | 1992 |

## the way it works

### In the future

When you are talking about something that is going to happen later on, then you are using the future tense. In French you can do this in two ways. You can use the verb **aller** with another verb in the infinitive, just as in English:

Cet après-midi, **je vais jouer** au golf. This afternoon I am going to play golf.

Alternatively, you can add the following endings to the infinitive of the verb to indicate the future:

| | | | |
|---|---|---|---|
| **-ai** | je jouer**ai** (I will play) | **-ons** | nous visiter**ons** (we will visit) |
| **-as** | tu donner**as** (you will give) | **-ez** | vous finir**ez** (you will finish) |
| **-a** | il écouter**a** (he will listen) | **-ont** | elles rencontrer**ont** (they will meet) |

Some verbs which end in **-e** drop the **-e** before adding the future endings:

attendre:    j'attendr**ai**                prendre:    elle prendr**a**
dire:         nous dir**ons**

There are quite a number of verbs which are irregular in the future and these have to be learned. Here are some common ones:

| | | | |
|---|---|---|---|
| aller: | j'**irai** | faire: | je **ferai** |
| avoir: | j'**aurai** | pouvoir: | je **pourrai** |
| être: | je **serai** | vouloir: | je **voudrai** |

### Negative expressions

In order to say *only, no one, never, nothing* and *no more* in French you have to use the negative expressions **ne . . . que, ne . . . personne, ne . . . jamais, ne . . . rien**, and **ne . . . plus**.

| | |
|---|---|
| Je **n'**ai **que** 40 francs. | I have only 40 francs. |
| Elle **ne** voit **personne**. | She sees no one (doesn't see anyone). |
| Tu **ne** vas **jamais** au cinéma. | You never go to the movies. |
| Vous **ne** dites **rien**. | You say nothing (don't say anything). |
| Je **n'**ai **plus** d'argent. | I have no more money. |
| Il **n'**est **plus** là. | He is no longer there. |

## things to do

**6.1** Say what you do and and don't like doing in your spare time. Use one of the following expressions: **J'aime bien/J'aime/Je n'aime pas/Je déteste**.

| *A la maison* | *Sports et loisirs* |
|---|---|
| 1 regarder la télé | 1 faire du vélo |
| 2 écouter la radio (listen to radio) | 2 jouer au tennis |
| 3 jouer aux cartes | 3 aller à la pêche |
| 4 faire du jardinage (garden) | 4 faire de la voile |
| 5 faire la cuisine (cook) | 5 faire du ski |

**6.2** And say what you think of each of the following. Use **ça me plaît, j'aime mieux/ça ne m'intéresse pas/ça m'ennuie/j'ai horreur de**

    1 le ballet—le théâtre—le cinéma—la musique classique
    2 le football—la natation—le cyclisme—la varappe

**3** Can you match the following questions and answers?

1 Elle habite seule? (*lives alone*)
2 Tu n'aimes pas les moules?
3 Encore 3 francs, s'il vous plaît.
4 Elles ne mangent pas de viande?
5 Tu n'as pas soif aujourd'hui?

(a) Non, elles ne mangent que des légumes et des fruits.
(b) Non, merci, je ne bois rien.
(c) Oui et elle ne voit personne.
(d) Non, je ne les mange jamais.
(e) Je m'excuse, je n'ai plus d'argent.

**4** Qu'est-ce que tu voudrais faire ce soir?
e.g., Tu aimerais aller au théâtre?  Oui, j'aimerais bien aller au théâtre.
Non, je ne peux pas sortir ce soir.

How would you deal with the following invitations?

1 Tu aimerais aller au match?
2 Tu as envie d'aller au cinéma?
3 Si on allait au centre des sports?
4 Ça te dirait d'aller à l'opéra?
5 Tu voudrais aller au musée?

**5** 1 Ask if there are any tickets for tonight's performance.
2 Ask if you can buy tickets for tonight's performance.
3 Ask if you can reserve two tickets in the balcony.
4 Ask if they give a discount for students.
5 Ask for three tickets on the ground floor with a discount for tomorrow.
6 Ask how much it comes to.

**6** 1 What is being advertised here?
2 What date does it close?
3 Where is it?
4 What time does it open and close?
5 Is it closed on Sundays?
6 What price are the tickets?

*Vocabulary*

la faïence    earthenware

---

**Expositions**

**400 ANS D'ART :
FAIENCES
ET PORCELAINES
DES PROVINCES
FRANÇAISES**

à l'abbaye de DAOULAS,
dans le Finistère (29224).

Jusqu'au 31 août 1987,
de 10 heures à 19 heures,
tous les jours sans exception.

Abbaye de Daoulas,
place de l'Église, 29224 Daoulas.
Entrée 25 F. Tél. 98.25.84.39.

## CONVERSATION

## *Talking about yourself/The weather*

### une réception

Patrick, Bernard, Martine and Sylvie have been invited to a reception on the last day of the trade fair.

| | |
|---|---|
| Bernard: | (to Patrick) **Je vous présente M. Alain Lemonnier, un collégue Lyonnais.** Patrick Vincent—Alain Lemonnier. |
| Patrick: | Enchanté de faire votre connaissance. |
| Bernard: | **Vous connaissez ma femme,** Martine? |
| Alain: | Non, pas encore. Enchanté, madame. |
| Patrick: | Vous êtes dessinateur aussi, Alain? |
| Alain: | Non, **je suis architecte.** |
| Patrick: | Ah, c'est intéressant. Ma fiancée fait ses études en architecture. Elle est étudiante à l'Université de Londres. |
| Bernard: | Ah, voilà Sylvie. Alain, **permettez-moi de vous présenter** Mlle Sylvie Corentin, une de nos meilleures programmeuses. **Elle travaille dans notre bureau à Rouen.** |
| Alain: | (to Martine) Et vous, madame **qu'est-ce que vous faites comme travail**? Vous êtes dans les affaires aussi? |
| Martine: | Non, je suis professeur dans une école maternelle. J'ai deux enfants, donc **Je travaille à mi-temps.** |
| Président: | (clearing his throat loudly) Mesdames et Messieurs, c'est un grand plaisir pour moi de vous accueillir ici ce soir. J'espère que tout le monde passera une soirée agréable . . . |

## un barbecue sur la plage/a beach barbecue

It is Sunday evening and the beach barbecue is in full swing.

Agathe: Quelle belle soirée. **Il fait toujours si beau temps** à S. Jean.
Henri: Oui, mais la météo prévoit des orages pour demain. La pluie va commencer pendant la nuit . . .
Agathe: Regarde les enfants. Ils s'amusent bien, n'est-ce pas?
(On another part of the beach . . . )
Thierry: Salut, Claire. Tiens, tu es anglaise! Tu habites à Londres?
Claire: Non, j'habite à Liverpool. Et toi?
Thierry: **Je vais au collège** à Tours. J'étudie pour devenir ingénieur.
Claire: **Et tu sais jouer de la guitare?**
Thierry: Oui, je joue dans un groupe à Tours. Dis, Claire, **Tu restes longtemps en France?**
Claire: Deux mois, environ.
Thierry: Et ça te plaît ici?
Claire: Oui, **ça me plaît beaucoup**. J'aime bien le soleil, et **il fait soleil tous les jours** à S. Jean-sur-Mer.

### Introductions

| | |
|---|---|
| **Je vous présente M. Alain Lemonnier.** | I'd like to introduce you to M. Alain Lemonnier. |
| **un collègue Lyonnais** | a colleague from Lyon |
| **Permettez-moi de vous présenter . . .** | Allow me to introduce . . . |
| **Laissez-moi vous présenter . . .** | Let me introduce . . . |
| **une de nos meilleures programmeuses** | one of our best computer programmers |
| **Elle travaille dans notre bureau à Rouen.** | She works in our Rouen office. |
| **Vous connaissez ma femme, Martine?** | Do you know my wife, Martine? |
| **Enchanté(e) de faire votre connaissance.** | Delighted to meet you. |
| **Enchanté(e), Madame.** | Delighted. |
| **Salut, Claire!** | Hello, Claire! |
| **C'est un grand plaisir pour moi de vous accueillir ici ce soir . . .** | It is a pleasure for me to welcome you here tonight . . . |

### Talking about jobs

| | |
|---|---|
| Que faites-vous (dans la vie)? | What do you do? |
| Qu'est-ce que vous faites comme travail? | What work do you do? |
| Vous êtes dessinateur aussi?* | Are you a designer too? |
| Vous êtes dans les affaires aussi? | Are you in business too? |
| Non, je suis architecte. | No, I'm an architect. |
| Je suis professeur dans une école maternelle. | I'm a teacher in a nursery school. |
| Ma fiancée fait ses études en architecture. | My fiancée is studying architecture. |
| Elle est étudiante à l'Université de Londres. | She's a student at London University. |
| J'étudie pour devenir ingénieur. | I'm studying to become an engineer. |
| Je suis étudiant(e). | I'm a student. |
| Je vais au collège. | I go to high school. |
| Je suis femme au foyer. | I'm a homemaker. |
| Je travaille chez moi/à la maison. | I work at home. |
| Je travaille à mi-temps. | I work part-time. |
| Je suis chômeur/se. | I'm unemployed. |

*Note in French, you leave out the equivalent of a/an when talking about your job.

### The weather

| | |
|---|---|
| le bulletin météorologique | weather forecast |
| la température | the temperature |
| une averse | shower |
| à l'ombre | in the shade |
| Quelle belle soirée. | What a lovely evening. |
| Il fait toujours si beau temps . . . | It's always so nice . . . |
| La météo prévoit des orages. | According to the forecast there are going to be storms. |
| La pluie va commencer pendant la nuit. | The rain will start during the night. |
| Il fait du soleil tous les jours. | It's sunny every day. |
| Quel temps fait-il? | What's the weather like? |
| Il fait beau temps/mauvais temps. | The weather is good/bad. |
| Il fait chaud/froid. | It's warm/cold. |
| Il fait du soleil. | It's sunny. |
| Le temps est ensoleillé. | It's sunny. |
| Le ciel se découvre. | It's clearing up. |
| Il est couvert/nuageux. | It's overcast/cloudy. |
| Il pleut/grêle. | It's raining/hailing. |
| Il fait du vent. | It's windy. |
| Il y a des orages. | It's stormy. |
| Il fait du brouillard/de la brume. | It's foggy/misty. |
| Il gèle/neige. | It's freezing/snowing. |

### Savez-vous jouer un instrument? (Can you play an instrument?)

| | |
|---|---|
| Tu sais jouer de la guitare? | Can you play the guitar? |
| Je joue du piano/du violon. | I play the piano/violin. |

## Talking about your stay

| | |
|---|---|
| Je suis ici en vacances/en voyage d'affaires/pour perfectionner la langue. | I'm here on vacation/on a business trip/to improve my French (the language). |
| Tu restes longtemps en France? | Are you staying long in France? |
| Combien de temps restez-vous en France? | How long are you staying in France? |
| Depuis combien de temps êtes-vous ici? | How long have you been here? |
| Deux mois, environ. | About two months. |
| six semaines/quinze jours | six weeks/two weeks |
| Je reste en France pendant huit jours | I'm staying in France for a week |
| Je suis ici depuis la fin de juillet/le mois dernier/la semaine dernière. | I've been here since the end of July/last month/last week. |
| C'est votre première visite ici? | Is it your first visit here? |
| Où logez-vous? | Where are you staying? |
| Ça te plaît ici? | Do you like it here? |
| Vous vous plaisez ici? | Do you like it here? |
| Oui, ça me plaît beaucoup. | Yes, very much. |
| Quand partez-vous? | When are you leaving? |
| Je pars demain/lundi/la semaine prochaine/le mois prochain/au début d'octobre. | I'm leaving tomorrow/on Monday/next week/next month/at the beginning of October. |

## USEFUL WORDS AND PHRASES

| | |
|---|---|
| pas encore | not yet |
| c'est intéressant | it's interesting |
| J'espère que tout le monde passera une soirée agréable. | I hope that everyone will have a pleasant evening. |
| Voilà Thierry qui arrive. | Here comes Thierry. |
| ce garçon-là | that boy |
| Tiens! | Well!/So! |

## the way it works

### Savoir and connaître

| savoir *to know* | | connaître *to know* | |
|---|---|---|---|
| je **sais** | nous **savons** | je **connais** | nous **connaissons** |
| tu **sais** | vous **savez** | tu **connais** | vous **connaissez** |
| il/elle **sait** | ils/elles **savent** | il/elle **connaît** | ils/elles **connaissent** |

**Savoir** and **connaître** both mean *to know* in French. Use **connaître** for knowing a person, a place, etc.:

| | |
|---|---|
| Vous connaissez ma femme, Martine? | Do you know my wife, Martine? |
| Je ne connais pas cette ville. | I don't know this town. |

**Savoir** is used for knowing how to do something, or knowing a fact (e.g., I know that . . . ):

| | |
|---|---|
| Tu sais jouer de la guitare? | Do know how to play the guitar? |
| Je sais que tu as raison. | I know you're right. |

### How to say bigger, better, etc.

To say something is bigger, smaller and so on, use **plus** together with the adjective, e.g.:

| | |
|---|---|
| **une grande** réception | a large reception |
| **une plus grande** réception | a larger reception |
| **la plus grande** réception | the largest reception |

The adjective "good" however is a bit different:

| | |
|---|---|
| **une bonne** programmeuse | a good programmer |
| **une meilleure** programmeuse | a better programmer |
| **la meilleure** programmeuse | the best programmer |

Note also how the adverb **bien** changes to **mieux**:

| | |
|---|---|
| Julien joue très **bien** de la guitare. | Julien plays the guitar very well. |
| Oui, mais Thierry joue **mieux**. | Yes, but Thierry plays better. |
| Mais moi, je joue **le mieux!** | But I play best! |

## things to do

**7.1** Everyone is talking about where they work and what they do. Answer the questions affirmatively, e.g., Vous travaillez dans une école?  Oui, je suis professeur. (See p. 83 for vocabulary.)

1 Vous travaillez dans un bureau?
2 Vous allez au collège?
3 Vous travaillez dans un hôpital?
4 Vous travaillez dans un garage?
5 Vous travaillez dans un magasin?
6 Vous travaillez dans une pharmacie?

**7.2** You are being asked about your visit to Belgium. Can you answer these questions in French?

1 D'où venez-vous, monsieur/madame? [Say that you come from London.]
2 Vous restez longtemps en Belgique? [You're staying about ten days.]
3 C'est votre première visite ici? [No, it's your second visit.]
4 Ça vous plaît à Bruxelles? [Yes, you like it very much.]
5 Alors, je vous invite à dîner demain soir.  [Thank him/her very much.]

**7.3** Quel temps fait-il aujourd'hui? Look at the weather map.

1 Quel temps fait-il à Rouen?
2 Quel temps fait-il à Lille?
3 Quel temps fait-il aux Alpes et aux Pyrénées?
4 Quelle est la température à Marseille?
5 Quelle est la température à Genève?

**4**                   *Le temps aujourd'hui*

«Il fera beau temps en général en France pendant le matin; toutefois, des nuages s'étendront\* progressivement aux régions du nord. Dans le sud, le temps restera chaud et il y aura beaucoup de soleil.

    L'après-midi sera agréable et légèrement moins\*\* chaud sur la Bretagne, le Nord, la Normandie et le Bassin parisien.

    Sur l'Aquitaine, le Massif Central et Midi-Pyrénées il y aura des orages très isolés dans la soirée et la nuit.

    Les températures atteindront 23°C à 28°F au nord de la Loire et 28°C à 30°C au sud; 32°C près des Pyrénées et en Provence.»

\* will spread    \*\* slightly less

1 According to the forecast, what will the weather be like in general during the morning?
2 What is likely to happen in the north, however?
3 In what way is this different from in the south?
4 What weather is forecast for Brittany in the afternoon?
5 Where and when are there likely to be scattered storms?
6 What temperatures are expected south of the Loire?

**5** See if you can fill in this form giving details about yourself in French.

---

**Nom** (last name).................................................................................
**Prénom** (first name) ............................................................................
**Date de naissance** (date of birth) .......................................................
**Lieu de naissance** (place of birth) ......................................................
**Signe astrologique** (sign of the zodiac) ..............................................
**Situation de famille** (marital status) ...................................................
[marié(e)/divorcé(e)/séparé(e)/célibataire; frère(s)/sœur(s)/
enfant(s)]\*
**Profession** .........................................................................................
**Lieu de travail** ..................................................................................
**Hobbies** ............................................................................................
**Sports préférés** .................................................................................
**Aime** .................................................................................................
**Déteste** .............................................................................................
**Rêve** (dream) .....................................................................................
**Angoisse** (worry/anxiety) ..................................................................
\* *Rayer la mention inutile* (delete where applicable)

---

# EXERCISE KEY

**1.1** 1 Bonjour, monsieur; au revoir, monsieur. 2 Bonjour, madame; au revoir, madame. 3 Bonjour, madame; au revoir, madame. 4 Bonjour, mademoiselle; au revoir, mademoiselle. 5 Salut, Damien!; au revoir, Damien.

**1.2** 1 Oui, je suis Madame Valéry. 2 Je m'appelle Monsieur/Madame . . . 3 Enchanté(e) de faire votre connaissance, madame. 4 Très bien merci, madame. 5 Ça va bien, merci.

**1.3** 1 Oui, c'est ma valise. 2 Oui, c'est mon taxi. 3 Oui, c'est ma voiture. 4 Oui, c'est mon fils. 5 Oui, c'est mon nom. 6 Oui, ce sont mes bagages. 7 Oui, c'est mon passeport.

**1.4** 1 salle de bains. 2 une chambre avec salle de bains et WC. 3 une chambre avec douche. 4 une chambre à deux lits. 5 une chambre à un grand lit. 6 une chambre à un lit. Elle voudrait une chambre à un grand lit, avec douche et cabinet de toilette.

**1.5** 2 Oui, la valise est dans le coffre. 3 Oui, la clé est dans la porte. 4 Oui, la tente est sous les arbres. 5 Oui, la douche est dans la salle de bains. 6 Oui, le passeport est dans le sac.

**1.6** 2 Non, elle n'est pas dans le coffre. 3 Non, elle n'est pas dans la porte. 4 Non, elle n'est pas sous les arbres. 5 Non, elle n'est pas dans la salle de bains. 6 Non, il n'est pas dans le sac.

**1.7** 2 Non, elle est petite. 3 Non, il est petit. 4 Non, il est petit. 5 Non, il est petit.

**1.8** 2 François, vous avez la chambre cinq au troisième étage. 3 Nathalie, vous avez la chambre dix au deuxième étage. 4 Christian, vous avez la chambre deux au rez-de-chaussée. 5 Florence, vous avez la chambre quatorze au quatrième étage.

**2.1** 1 Je voudrais du café et des croissants. 2 Je voudrais du pain, du beurre, de la confiture et du thé. 3 Je voudrais une tasse de thé. 4 Je voudrais un jus d'orange et un yaourt. 5 Je voudrais du thé avec du pain et du beurre.

**2.2** 1 trois heures moins cinq or deux heures cinquante-cinq. 2 trois heures cinq. 3 trois heures et quart. 4 trois heures moins le quart or deux heures quarante-cinq. 5 une heure. 6 trois heures vingt.

**2.3** You: A quelle heure est le prochain train pour Paris?
You: Combien de temps faut-il pour aller de Boulogne à Paris?
You: Le train arrive à quelle heure?
You: Faut-il changer?

**2.4** 2 Il voudrait un (billet) aller simple à Lyon, en première class. 3 Ils voudraient deux (billets) aller-retour à Avignon, en deuxième classe. 4 Il voudrait un (billet) aller-retour à Bordeaux, en deuxième classe. 5 Ils voudraient deux (billets) aller simple à Nice, en première classe.

**2.5** e.g. (a) Pour aller à la gare, s.v.p? (b) Où est le parc? (c) Est-ce qu'il y a un restaurant près d'ici? (d) Où est la rue du Port, s.v.p? (e) Où est la poste, s.v.p? (f) S'il vous plaît, monsieur, la station de métro? (g) Pour aller à la plage, s.v.p? (h) Pour aller à l'hôtel, s.v.p? (i) S'il vous plaît, madame, où est l'arrêt d'autobus? (j) Est-ce qu'il y a une boulangerie près d'ici?

**2.6** 1 le stade. 2 la banque. 3 le cinéma. 4 la bibliothèque. 5 le syndicat d'initiative. 6 le théâtre.

**3.1** 1 (b). 2 (c). 3 (a). 4 (e). 5 (d). 6 (h). 7 (f). 8 (g).

**3.2** Je n'aime pas la couleur. Pouvez-vous me montrer une autre couleur—gris ou brun, peut-être? . . . Ce blouson est trop grand. Avez-vous quelque chose de petit? . . . Oui, s'il vous plaît. Il me va bien. C'est combien? . . . Je le prends.

**3.3** Non, elle est trop petite. . . . Non, elle est trop grande. . . . Non, il est trop court. . . . Non, il est trop long. . . . Non, elles sont trop petites.

**3.4** 1 (e). 2 (d). 3 (b). 4 (a). 5 (c).

**3.5** 250 grams of butter, a piece of cheese, ½ kilo of granulated sugar, a liter of milk, 200 grams of paté, 4 slices of ham, a can of fish soup, a kilo of apples, a pound of pears, ½ liter of vinegar, 100 grams of Russian salad, a carton of grated carrots, a container of ground coffee, 2 bottles of red wine, a dozen eggs.

**3.6** Deux baguettes, s.v.p. . . . Je voudrais aussi quatre croissants, deux brioches et une tarte aux pommes. . . . C'est combien?

**3.7** *(starting from top left going clockwise)* Pour monsieur, les huîtres, et après, un bifteck avec des pommes frites, et un verre de vin rouge. Pour madame, l'assiette de fruits de mer et du poulet, avec du vin blanc—pas de pommes de terre. Pour monsieur, des cuisses de grenouille, du porc, et une bière. Et apportez-lui une salade verte avec le porc, s.v.p. Pour mademoiselle, une tarte aux pommes, une glace et un cola. Pour monsieur des frites et un jus d'orange. Pour madame le consommé, et après la truite. Et à boire, une bouteille d'eau minérale, s.v.p.

**3.8** Example: Je prends un croque-monsieur, s.v.p. . . . Un café crème. Je prends un hamburger, s.v.p. . . . Une pression.

**4.1** 1 (b), 2 (c), 3 (e), 4 (a), 5 (f), 6 (d).

**4.2** Celui-ci, s'il vous plaît. Celle-là, s'il vous plaît. Celui-ci, s'il vous plaît. Celui-ci et celui-là, s'il vous plaît.

**4.3** Je voudrais des timbres, s'il vous plaît. Je voudrais envoyer une lettre et deux cartes postales. La lettre est pour l'Angleterre, et les cartes postales sont pour les Etats-Unis. Non, je voudrais (aussi) envoyer un colis à Paris.

**4.4** 1 Quel est le taux de change aujourd'hui? 2 Est-ce que je peux encaisser un chèque? 3 Je voudrais encaisser cinquante dollars de chèques de voyage. 4 Je voudrais changer un billet de cent francs pour dix pièces de dix francs.

**4.5** C'est bien le 87-23-25? Je voudrais parler à M. Lotte, s'il vous plaît. C'est . . . Est-ce qu'il peut me téléphoner?/Pouvez-vous lui dire de me téléphoner? C'est le numéro . . . Au revoir, madame.

**4.6** 2 Bernard lui dit ''Bonjour.'' 3 Le caissier lui donne un billet de 100F. 4 Elle lui téléphone. 5 Elle leur écrit.

**5.1** 1 Il a mal au dos. 2 Il a mal à la tête. 3 Il a mal aux oreilles. 4 Il a mal au doigt. 5 Il a mal au ventre. 6 Il a mal à la jambe.

**5.2** 1 (b), 2 (c), 3 (c), 4 (a).

**5.3** (a) Faites le plein, s'il vous plaît. (b) Je voudrais/Donnez-moi vingt-cinq litres d'essence super, s'il vous plaît. (c) Donnez-moi de l'huile. (d) Donnez-moi de l'eau pour la batterie. (e) Je voudrais vérifier la pression des pneus.

**5.4** (a) Je suis en panne. (b) Ma voiture ne démarre pas. (c) Mes freins ne marchent pas. Est-ce que vous avez un service de dépannage? Je suis pressé(e)—je suis déjà en retard.

**5.5** 1 (b). 2 (a) Votre/Mon nom et votre/mon adresse, (b) votre permis de conduire, (c) votre police d'assurance, (d) un constat. 3 (c).

**6.1** *A la maison:* e.g., J'aime écouter la radio, j'aime faire du jardinage, je n'aime pas faire la cuisine, je déteste regarder la télé. *Sports et loisirs:* e.g., J'aime bien faire du vélo, j'aime aller à la pêche, je n'aime pas faire du ski, je déteste faire de la voile.

**6.2** e.g., 1 Ça me plaît, le ballet. Ça m'ennuie, la musique classique. Ça ne m'intéresse pas, le cinéma. J'ai horreur du théâtre.

**6.3** 1 (c). 2 (d). 3 (e). 4 (a). 5 (b).

**6.4** e.g., 1 Non, ça ne m'intéresse pas le football. 2 Oui, je voudrais bien y aller. 3 Non, je ne peux pas sortir ce matin. 4 Oh non, j'ai horreur de l'opéra. 5 Oui, avec plaisir.

**6.5** 1 Y a-t-il des places pour ce soir? 2 Peut-on acheter des billets pour le spectacle? 3 Je voudrais réserver deux places au balcon. 4 Y a-t-il des réductions pour les étudiants? 5 Je voudrais trois billets à l'orchestre avec réduction pour demain. 6 Ça fait combien, s.v.p?

**6.6** 1 An exhibition of French china. 2 August 31. 3 Daoulas Abbey, Finistère. 4 Opens 10 a.m., closes 7 p.m. 5 No. 6 25 F.

**7.1** 1 Oui, je suis secrétaire/ journaliste/programmeur/se, etc. 2 Oui, je suis étudiant(e). 3 Oui, je suis médecin/infirmière. 4 Oui, je suis

mécanicien. 5 Oui, je suis vendeur/se.
6 Oui, je suis pharmacien(ne).
**7.2** 1 Je viens de Londres. 2 Dix jours
environ. 3 Non, c'est ma deuxième
visite. 4 Oui, ça me plaît beaucoup.
5 Merci beaucoup, monsieur/madame.
**7.3** 1 Il fait du soleil. 2 Il est nuageux.

3 Il y a des orages. 4 31°, 5 26°.
**7.4** 1 Fine. 2 Clouds will spread to the
north. 3 It will stay warm and sunny in
the south. 4 Pleasant and slightly less
warm. 5 Aquitaine, the Massif Central
and the Midi-Pyrenees. 6 28° to 30°.

## English–French topic vocabularies

### Numbers 1–99

### Numbers 100–1000

| | | | | | | | |
|---|---|---|---|---|---|---|---|
| 1 | un, une | 19 | dix-neuf | 80 | quatre-vingts | 100 | cent |
| 2 | deux | 20 | vingt | | (4 × 20) | 101 | cent un |
| 3 | trois | 21 | vingt et un | 81 | quatre-vingt-un | 150 | cent cinquante |
| 4 | quatre | 22 | vingt-deux | 90 | quatre-vingt-dix | 200 | deux cents |
| 5 | cinq | 23 | vingt-trois | 99 | quatre-vingt-dix- | 210 | deux cent dix |
| 6 | six | 24 | vingt-quatre | | neuf | 250 | deux cent |
| 7 | sept | 25 | vingt-cinq | | | | cinquante |
| 8 | huit | 26 | vingt-six | | | 300 | trois cents |
| 9 | neuf | 27 | vingt-sept | first | premier/ | 400 | quatre cents |
| 10 | dix | 28 | vingt-huit | | ère | 500 | cinq cents |
| 11 | onze | 29 | vingt-neuf | second | deuxième | 600 | six cents |
| 12 | douze | 30 | trente | third | troisième | 700 | sept cents |
| 13 | treize | 31 | trente et un | fourth | quatrième | 800 | huit cents |
| 14 | quatorze | 32 | trente-deux | fifth | cinquième | 900 | neuf cents |
| 15 | quinze | | etc. | sixth | sixième | 1000 | mille |
| 16 | seize | 40 | quarante | seventh | septième | | |
| 17 | dix-sept | 50 | cinquante | eighth | huitième | | |
| 18 | dix-huit | 60 | soixante | ninth | neuvième | | |
| | | 70 | soixante-dix | tenth | dixième | | |

### Months/les mois

### Seasons/les saisons

| | | | | | |
|---|---|---|---|---|---|
| January | janvier | July | juillet | Spring | le printemps |
| February | février | August | août | Summer | l'été |
| March | mars | September | septembre | Autumn | l'automne |
| April | avril | October | octobre | Winter | l'hiver |
| May | mai | November | novembre | | |
| June | juin | December | décembre | | |

### Clothes

| | | | |
|---|---|---|---|
| belt | la ceinture | pajamas | le pyjama |
| blouse | le chemisier | pants | le pantalon |
| bra | le soutien-gorge | raincoat | l'imperméable (m) |
| coat | le manteau | scarf | l'écharpe (f) |
| dress | la robe | shirt | la chemise |
| gloves | les gants | skirt | la jupe |
| handbag | le sac à main | socks | les chaussettes (f) |
| hat | le chapeau | stockings | les bas |
| jacket | la veste, le blouson | suit (men's) | le complet |
| jeans | le jean | suit (women's) | le tailleur |
| nightgown | la chemise de nuit | sweatsuit | le survêtement |
| overalls | la blouse | swimsuit | le maillot de bain |

# VOCABULARY

| | | | |
|---|---|---|---|
| T-shirt | le tee-shirt | underpants | le slip |
| tights | le collant | vest | le gilet |

## Colors

| | |
|---|---|
| black | noir |
| blue | bleu |
| brown | marron, brun |
| green | vert |
| grey | gris |
| pink | rose |
| red | rouge |
| white | blanc(he) |
| yellow | jaune |
| dark | foncé |
| light | clair |

## Materials

| | |
|---|---|
| cotton | le coton |
| leather | le cuir |
| nylon | le nylon |
| silk | la soie |
| straw | la paille |
| wool | la laine |
| velvet | le velours |

## At the pharmacy/à la pharmacie

| | | | |
|---|---|---|---|
| adhesive bandage | le sparadrap | comb | le peigne |
| bandage | le tricostéril | condoms | les préservatifs |
| capsule | la gélule | disposable diapers | les couches d'enfant |
| medicine | le médicament | perfume | le parfum |
| ointment | la pommade | razor blades | les lames de rasoir |
| pill, tablet | le comprimé | sanitary napkins | les serviettes |
| pharmacy on duty | la pharmacie de service | | hygiéniques |
| prescription | l'ordonnance | shampoo | le shampooing |
| sleeping pill | le somnifère | shaving cream | la crème à raser |
| suppository | le suppositoire | soap (unscented) | le savon (non parfumé) |
| | | suntan oil | l'huile solaire |
| | | suntan cream | la crème solaire |

### Toiletries

| | | | |
|---|---|---|---|
| baby food | l'alimentation pour enfants | tampons | les tampons hygiéniques |
| | | toothbrush | la brosse à dents |
| brush | la brosse | toothpaste | le dentifrice |

## Shopping for food

### Fish/les poissons

| | | | |
|---|---|---|---|
| cod | la morue/le cabillaud | snails | les escargots |
| clams | les palourdes | sole fillets | les filets de sole |
| crab | le crabe | trout | la truite |
| crayfish | les écrevisses | | |
| hake | le colin | | |

### Meat/les viandes

| | | | |
|---|---|---|---|
| herring | le hareng | beef | le bœuf |
| lobster | le homard | ham | le jambon |
| monkfish | la lotte | ground meat | la viande hachée |
| mussels | les moules | kidneys | les rognons |
| oysters | les huîtres | lamb | l'agneau |
| prawns | les langoustines | pork | le porc |
| salmon | le saumon | sausages | les saucisses |
| shrimps | les crevettes | steak | le bifteck/le steak |
| skate | la raie | veal | le veau |

## Poultry/la volaille

| | |
|---|---|
| chicken | le poulet |
| duck | le canard |
| duckling | le caneton |
| pheasant | le faisan |

## Vegetables/les légumes

| | |
|---|---|
| asparagus | l'asperge |
| cabbage | le chou |
| cauliflower | le chou-fleur |
| carrot | la carotte |
| celery | le céleri |
| cucumber | le concombre |
| endive | l'endive |
| french fries | les frites |
| garlic | l'ail |
| green beans | les haricots verts |
| kidney beans | les flageolets |
| leek | le poireau |
| lettuce | la laitue |
| mushroom | le champignon |
| onion | l'oignon |
| peas | les petits pois |
| pepper | le poivron (vert) |
| potato | la pomme de terre |
| spinach | les épinards |
| tomato | la tomate |

## At the bakery/à la boulangerie

| | |
|---|---|
| bread, loaf | le pain |
| French bread | la baguette |
| long, thin loaf | la ficelle |
| large loaf | le gros pain |
| whole wheat bread | le pain complet |
| crescent roll | le croissant |
| brioche | la brioche |
| apricot pie | la tarte aux abricots |
| apple pie | la tarte aux pommes |
| raisin bread | le pain au raisin |

## Fruit/les fruits

| | |
|---|---|
| apple | la pomme |
| apricot | l'abricot |
| banana | la banane |
| blackcurrant | le cassis |
| cherry | la cerise |
| grape(s) | le raisin |
| grapefruit | le pamplemousse |
| lemon | le citron |
| orange | l'orange |
| peach | la pêche |
| pear | la poire |
| pineapple | l'ananas |
| plum | la prune |
| raspberry | la framboise |
| strawberry | la fraise |

## Other groceries

| | |
|---|---|
| butter | le beurre |
| cheese | le fromage |
| coffee | le café |
| cookies | les biscuits |
| flour | la farine |
| margarine | la margarine |
| milk | le lait |
| oil | l'huile |
| pasta | les pâtes |
| rice | le riz |
| sugar | le sucre |
| tea | le thé |

## Cooking terms

| | |
|---|---|
| baked | au four |
| boiled | bouilli |
| fried | frit |
| grilled | grillé |
| smoked | fumé |
| steamed | à la vapeur |
| roast | rôti |

## Sports and games

| | |
|---|---|
| to do | faire du/de la/de l' |
| aerobics | l'aérobic |
| archery | le tir à l'arc |
| climbing | l'alpinisme/la varappe |
| cycling | le vélo |
| dancing | la danse |
| fishing | la pêche |
| riding | l'équitation |
| sailing | la voile |
| shooting | la chasse |
| skating | le patinage |
| skiing | le ski |
| swimming | la natation |
| walking | la randonnée |
| waterskiing | le ski nautique |

## Equipment

| | |
|---|---|
| fishing rod | la canne à pêche |
| racket | la racquette |
| sailboat | le bateau à voile |
| skates | les patins |
| skis | les skis |
| ski boots | les chaussures de ski |
| windsurfer | la planche à voile |

# VOCABULARY

## Parts of the body

| | | | |
|---|---|---|---|
| ankle | la cheville | throat | la gorge |
| arm | le bras | toe | le doigt de pied |
| back | le dos | tooth | la dent |
| chest | la poitrine | wrist | le poignet |
| ear | l'oreille | | |

## Parts of the car

| | | | |
|---|---|---|---|
| elbow | le coude | battery | la batterie |
| eye | l'œil | brakes | les freins |
| eyes | les yeux | bulbs | les ampoules |
| face | la figure/le visage | clutch | l'embrayage |
| finger | le doigt | distributor | le distributeur |
| foot | le pied | engine | le moteur |
| hair | les cheveux | exhaust | le tuyau d'échappement |
| hand | la main | fan belt | la courroie du ventilateur |
| head | la tête | gas tank | le réservoir d'essence |
| heart | le cœur | gears | les vitesses |
| hip | la hanche | headlights | les phares |
| knee | le genou | ignition | l'allumage |
| leg | la jambe | radiator | le radiateur |
| lip | la lèvre | spark plugs | les bougies |
| mouth | la bouche | steering wheel | le volant |
| neck | le cou | tires | les pneus |
| nose | le nez | turn signal | l'indicateur |
| skin | la peau | wheels | les roues |
| small of back | les reins | windshield | le pare-brise |
| stomach | le ventre | windshield wipers | les essuie-glace |
| thigh | la cuisse | | |

## Professions

| | | | |
|---|---|---|---|
| accountant | comptable | sales rep | représentant |
| artist | artiste | secretary | secrétaire |
| banker | banquier | social worker | assistant/e social/e |
| bank teller | employé/e de banque | | |
| builder | maçon | | |
| businessman | homme d'affaires | | |

### Workplaces

| | | | |
|---|---|---|---|
| businesswoman | femme d'affaires | I work in . . . | Je travaille dans . . . |
| chef | cuisiner/ière | a bank | une banque |
| civil servant | fonctionnaire | a clinic | une clinique |
| company director | directeur/trice | a factory | une fabrique (small); une usine (large) |
| computer programmer | programmeur/euse | a firm | une maison de commerce/une firme |
| computer operator | opérateur/trice | a garage | un garage |
| dentist | dentiste | a high school | un collège |
| doctor | médecin | a hospital | un hôpital |
| hairdresser | coiffeur/euse | a laboratory | un laboratoire |
| IBM executive | cadre de IBM | an office | un bureau |
| interpreter | interprète | a store | un magasin |
| journalist | journaliste | a studio | un studio |
| lawyer | avocat | a workshop | un atelier |
| mechanic | mécanicien | | |
| nurse | infirmière | | |
| pharmacist | pharmacien/ne | | |
| policeman | agent de police | | |
| real estate agent | agent immobilière | | |

# VOCABULARY

## French-English Vocabulary

**à** at; **—point** medium (steak)
**abbaye** *f.* abbey
**accord: d'—** OK, all right
**accrochage** *m.* collision
**accueillir** welcome
**acheter** buy
**addition** *f.* check (restaurant)
**adorer** love
**adresse** *f.* address
**aéroport** *m.* airport
**affaires** *f. pl.* business
**affreux/se** awful
**âge** *m.* age
**agent** *(m.)* **de police** police officer
**agneau** *m.* lamb
**agréable** pleasant
**aider** help
**ail** *m.* garlic
**aimer** like; **—mieux** prefer
**alcool** *m.* alcohol
**alimentation** *f.* grocery story
**aller** *(m.)* **simple** one-way (ticket)
**aller-retour** *m.* round-trip (ticket)
**aller** go; feel; suit
**alors** well, then
**ambulance** *f.* ambulance
**ami(e)** *m., f.* friend
**amour** *m.* love
**s'amuser** enjoy o.self
**an** *m.,* **année** *f.* year
**annuaire** *m.* telephone book
**annuel/le** annual
**appareil** *m.* telephone;
   **—photo** camera
**appeler** call; **s'—** be named
**apporter** bring
**après** after
**après-midi** afternoon
**arbre** *m.* tree
**architecte** *m.* architect
**argent** *m.* money
**s'arranger** be settled
**arrêt** *(m.)* **d'autobus** bus stop
**arriver** arrive; happen
**ascenseur** *m.* elevator
**assez** enough, quite
**s'asseoir** sit down
**assiette** *f.* plate, dish
**assister (à)** be present (at)
**assurance** *f.* insurance
**atteindre** reach

**attendre** wait for
**au-dessous** below
**au-dessus** above
**auberge** *(f.)* **de jeunesse** youth hostel
**aujourd'hui** today
**au revoir** good-bye
**aussi** too, as well
**autre** other
**auto** *m.* car
**autobus** *m.* bus
**autoroute** *f.* highway
**avance: à l'—** in advance; **d'—** early
**avec** with
**averse** *f.* shower (rain)
**avion** *m.* airplane
**avis: à mon—** in my opinion
**avoir** have

**bagages** *m. pl.* luggage
**balcon** *m.* balcony
**banane** *f.* banana
**banque** *f.* bank
**barquette** *f.* carton
**bateau** *m.* boat
**batiment** *m.* building
**beau, belle, bel** beautiful, good, etc.
**beaucoup** very much; a lot
**besoin: avoir—de** need
**beurre** *m.* butter
**bicyclette** *f.* bicycle
**bien** well; **—sûr** of course
**bientôt** soon
**bière** *f.* beer
**bifteck** *m.* steak
**billet** *m.* ticket; bill (money)
**blanc(he)** white
**blessé** hurt, injured
**bleu** blue; very rare; *(m.)* bruise
**blouson** *m.* (short) jacket
**bœuf** *m.* beef
**boire** drink
**bois** *m.* wood
**boisson** *f.* drink
**boîte** *f.* box, can; **—aux lettres**
   mailbox; **—de nuit** night club
**bon(ne)** good; **—marché** cheap
**bonjour** hello
**de bonne heure** early
**boucherie** *f.* butcher shop
**boulangerie** *f.* bakery
**bouteille** *f.* bottle
**bras** *m.* arm
**brosse** *f.* brush

# VOCABULARY

**brouillard** *m.* fog
**brume** *f.* mist
**brun** brown
**Bruxelles** Brussels
**bureau** *m.* office; **—de change**
currency exchange; **—de poste**
post office; **—de tabac** tobacco store
**bulletin** *(m.)* **météorologique**
weather forecast

**ça** that
**cabine** *(f.)* **téléphonique** phone booth
**cabinet** *(m.)* **de toilette** toilet
**café** *m.* coffee, café
**caisse** *f.* cashier
**caisser** *m.* cashier
**calmant** *m.* painkiller
**se calmer** calm down
**campagne** *f.* country
**camarade** *m., f.* friend
**camion** *m.* truck
**camping** *m.* camping, campground
**car** *m.* bus, coach
**carafe** *f.* jug
**caravane** *f.* trailer
**carnet** *m.* book of tickets; **—de**
**chèques** checkbook; **—de**
**timbres** book of stamps
**carotte** *f.* carrot
**carrefour** *m.* crossroads
**carte** *f.* menu, map, card;
**—bancaire** bank card;
**—de crédit** credit card; **—postale**
postcard; **—des vins** wine list
**cas** *m.* case
**cassé** broken
**casse-croûte** *m.* snack
**catastrophe** *f.* catastrophe
**cause: à—de** because of
**ce cette, cet** this, that
**cela** that
**celui-ci** this one; **celui-là** that one
**centre** *m.* center
**cerise** *f.* cherry
**ces** these, those
**c'est** it is
**chambre** *f.* room
**changer** change, exchange
**chapeau** *m.* hat
**chaque** each
**charcuterie** *f.* delicatessen
**chariot** *m.* cart
**chasser** chase
**château** *m.* castle

**chaud** warm
**chaussures** *f. pl.* shoes
**chemin** *m.* way, road; **—de**
**fer** railroad
**chemise** *f.* shirt
**chemisier** *m.* blouse
**chèque** *m.* check; **—s de voyage/**
**travellers** traveler's checks
**cher/chère** expensive, dear
**chercher** look for
**chéri(e)** *m., f.* darling
**chez** at the home of
**chic** smart
**chocolat** *m.* chocolate
**choisir** choose
**choix** *f.* choice
**chômeur/se** *m.,f.* unemployed person
**chose** *f.* thing
**cidre** *m.* cider
**ciel** *m.* sky
**cigarette** *f.* cigarette
**cinéma** *m.* movies
**circulation** *f.* traffic
**citron** *m.* lemon
**classe** *f.* class
**clé** *f.* key
**cœur** *m.* heart
**coffre** *m.* trunk
**coiffeur** *m.* hairdresser
**colis** *m.* parcel
**collège** *m.* high school
**collègue** *m., f.* colleague
**combien** how much, how many
**commander** order
**comme** as, like
**commencer** begin
**comment** how
**commissariat** *(m.)* **de police** police
station
**complet** full; **—***(m.)* man's suit
**complètement** completely
**comprendre** understand
**comprimé** *m.* tablet, pill
**compris** included
**concert** *m.* concert
**conducteur/trice** *m., f.* driver
**confiserie** *f.* candy store
**confiture** *f.* jam
**confortable** comfortable
**connaissance** *f.* acquaintance
**connaître** know
**conseiller** advise
**consigne** *f.* luggage storage;
**—automatique** locker

**constat** *m.* accident report
**consulter** consult
**continuer** continue
**contravention** *f.* fine
**contre** against
**copain** *m.*, **copine** *f.* friend, pal
**correspondance** *f.* connection
**côte** *f.* coast; rib
**côté: à—de** next to, beside
**côtelette** *f.* chop, cutlet
**coton** *m.* cotton
**cou** *m.* neck
**se coucher** go to bed
**couleur** *f.* color
**coupé** cut
**courrier** *m.* mail
**court** short
**cousin(e)** *m.*, *f.* cousin
**couteau** *m.* knife
**coûter** cost
**couvert** overcast, covered;
 **—(m.)** place setting
**couverture** *f.* blanket
**crème** *f.* cream
**crémerie** *f.* dairy
**crevettes** *f. pl.* shrimps
**crise** *f.* crisis; **—de foie** upset stomach
**croire** think, believe
**cuillère** *f.* spoon
**cuisine** *f.* kitchen; **faire la—** cook
**cuisiner** cook
**cuisinier/ière** *m.*, *f.* cook
**cuir** *m.* leather

**dame** *f.* lady
**danger** *m.* danger
**dans** in
**danse** *f.* dance
**de** of, from; some, any
**début** *m.* beginning
**défendu, défense de** forbidden (to)
**déjà** already
**déjeuner** *m.* lunch; **petit—** breakfast
**demain** tomorrow
**demander** ask for
**démarrer** start (car)
**demi** half; **—heure** *f.* half an hour;
 **—pension** *f.* half board
**dent** *f.* tooth
**dentifrice** *m.* toothpaste
**dentiste** *m.*, *f.* dentist
**départ** *m.* departure
**se dépêcher** hurry
**depuis** since

**dernier/ère** last
**des** some, any
**descendre** get off, go down
**désirer** want
**désolé** sorry
**dessert** *m.* dessert
**dessinateur** *m.* designer
**destination** *f.* destination
**détester** hate, detest
**devenir** become
**devoir** have to, must
**Dieu** *m.* God
**difficile** difficult
**dîner** *m.* dinner, supper; **— dine**
**dire** say
**direction** *f.* direction
**discuter** discuss
**disque** *(m.)* **de stationnement**
 parking disk
**docteur** *m.* doctor
**doigt** *m.* finger
**dommage** *m.* pity, shame
**donner** give
**dormir** sleep
**dos** *m.* back
**douane** *f.* customs
**douche** *f.* shower
**douloureux/se** painful
**doute: sans—** no doubt
**douzaine** *f.* dozen
**dresser** put up (tent)
**droguerie** *f.* hardware store
**droite** right
**du, de la, de l'** some, any

**eau** *f.* water
**école** *f.* school
**écrevisse** *f.* crayfish, prawn
**écrire** write
**égal: ça m'est—** I don't care;
 **également** equally, likewise
**église** *f.* church
**elle** she
**emballer** wrap (up)
**emmener** take
**emplacement** *m.* campsite
**employé(e)** *m.*, *f.* employee;
 **—de banque** bank teller
**en** in; some
**encaisser** cash (check)
**enfant** *m.*, *f.* child
**ennuyer** bore
**entrée** *f.* entrance
**entrer** enter

# VOCABULARY

environ  around about
envoyer  send
erreur *f.*  mistake
escalier *m.*  staircase
escargot *m.*  snail
espérer  hope
essayer  try (on)
essence *f.*  gas
étage *m.*  story, floor
étroit  tight, narrow
étudiant(e) *m., f.*  student
étudier  study
études: faire des—  study
envie: avoir—de  want
exposition *f.*  exhibition

face: en—de  across from
faim *f.*  hunger; avoir—  be hungry
faire  do, make; —beau  be nice
  (weather); ça fait  that comes to
farine *f.*  flour
faut: il—  be necessary, (I etc.) must
faute *f.*  fault
femme *f.*  woman, wife
fermer  close; fermé  closed
fermeture *f.*  closure
feux *m. pl.*  traffic lights
fiche *f.*  form
fièvre *f.*  fever, temperature
filet *m.*  net
fille *f.*  girl, daughter
film *m.*  film; —policier  thriller
fils *m.*  son
fin *f.*  end
finir  finish
flatteur/se  flattering
foie *m.*  liver
fois *f.*  time
forêt *f.*  forest
formulaire *m.*  form
fourchette *f.*  fork
frais/fraîche  fresh
fréquent  frequent
fraise *f.*  strawberry
framboise *f.*  raspberry
freins *m. pl.*  brakes
frites *f. pl.*  french fries
froid  cold
fromage *m.*  cheese
fruit *m.*  fruit
fumer  smoke

gâché  ruined
galerie, seconde *f.*  second balcony

garage *m.*  garage
garçon *m.*  boy, waiter
gardien/ne *m., f.*  warden
gare *f.*  station
gasoil *m.*  diesel
gâteau *m.*  cake
gauche  left
gaz *m.*  gas
geler  freeze
général: en—  in general
genou(x) *m. (pl.)*  knee(s)
gentil(le)  nice, kind
gilet *m.*  jacket, vest
glace *f.*  ice cream; glass
gonflé  swollen
gorge *f.*  throat
gourmand  greedy
goût *m.*  taste
goûter  taste; —(m.)  afternoon snack
gramme *m.*  gram
grand  large, big; —s magasins *m. pl.*
  department store; —mère *f.*
  grandmother; —père *m.*
  grandfather
gratuit  free
grave  serious
grêle *f.*  hail
grenouille *f.*  frog
gris  grey
grillé  grilled
gueule *(f.)* de bois  hangover
guichet *m.*  ticket office, counter
guide *m.*  guide, guidebook
guitare *f.*  guitar

habiter  live
heure *f.*  hour; —s  o'clock; —s
  d'ouverture  opening hours
heureux/se  happy, fortunate
hier  yesterday
homard *m.*  lobster
homme *m.*  man
hôpital *f.*  hospital
horaire *m.*  schedule
horreur: avoir—de  hate
hors d'œuvre *m.*  appetizer
hôtel *m.*  hotel; —de ville  town hall
huile *f.*  oil; —solaire  suntan lotion
huître *f. pl.*  oysters

ici  here
idée *f.*  idea
idiot  stupid
il  he, it; —y a  there is, there are

île *f.*  island
immédiatement  immediately
imperméable *m.*  raincoat
infirmière *f.*  nurse
s'inquiéter  worry, be worried
instant *m.*  moment, instant
instrument *m.*  instrument
intéressant  interesting
intéresser  interest; s'—(à)  be
  interested (in)
interdit, interdiction de  forbidden (to)
isolé  isolated
inviter  invite

jambe *f.*  leg
jambon *m.*  ham
jardin *m.*  garden
jeton *m.*  token
joindre  join, enclose
joli  pretty
jouer  play, show (film)
jour *m.*  day; —s fériés  (public)
  holidays; tous les —s  every day
journal *m.*  newspaper
jupe *f.*  skirt
jus *m.*  juice
jusqu'à  to, until
juste  just, right

kilo *m.*  kilo(gram)
kiosque *m.*  newsstand

la  the, it
là  there; —bas  over there
lac *m.*  lake
laine *f.*  wool
laisser  leave
lait *m.*  milk
laitue *f.*  lettuce
lame *(f.)* à raser  razor blade
langoustine *f.*  prawn
langue *f.*  language; tongue
le  the, it
légumes *m. pl.*  vegetables
lent  slow; lentement  slowly
les  the, them
lettre *f.*  letter
leur  their
se lever  get up
librairie *f.*  bookstore
libre  free; —service  self-service
ligne *f.*  line
limonade *f.*  soda
lire  read

litre *m.*  liter
livre *f.*  pound; —*(m.)*  book
location *f.* (de voitures)  (car) rental
loin  far
Londres  London
long(ue)  long
longer  go along
longtemps  long, a long time
louer  rent
lumière *f.*  light
lunettes *f. pl.*  glasses

ma  my
madame  madam, Mrs.
mademoiselle  Miss
magasin *m.*  shop
maillot *(m.)* de bain  bathing suit
main *f.*  hand
maintenant  now
mairie *f.*  town hall
mais  but
maison *f.*  house, home; —de
  commerce  firm
mal: j'ai—à . . .  my . . . hurts
malade  ill
maladroit  clumsy
manger  eat
manteau *m.*  coat
marchand(e) *m., f.*  vendor
marché *m.*  market
marcher  walk, work (function)
mari *m.*  husband
marron  (chestnut) brown
match *m.* (de football)  (soccer) game
matin *m.*  morning
mauvais  bad
médecin *m.*  doctor
médicament *m.*  medicine
meilleur  better, best
menu *m.*  set meal, fixed-price menu
mer *f.*  sea
merci  thank you
mère *f.*  mother
message *m.*  message
messieurs *m.*  gentlemen
mesurer  measure
météo *f.*  forecast
mètre *m.*  meter
métro *m.*  subway
midi  noon
mieux  better
minuit  midnight
minute *f.*  minute
mode: à la—  fashionable

# VOCABULARY

**moi** me
**moins** less
**mois** *m.* month
**mon, ma, mes** my
**monnaie** *f.* change
**monsieur** *m.* gentleman, Mr.
**montagne** *f.* mountain
**monter** go up
**montre** *f.* watch
**montrer** show
**morceau** *m.* piece
**morue** *f.* cod
**mouchoir** *m.* handkerchief
**moules** *f. pl.* mussels
**moulu** ground
**musée** *m.* museum; **−d'art** art gallery
**musique** *f.* music

**nager** swim
**nationalité** *f.* nationality
**nature** plain
**ne . . . jamais** never; **ne . . . pas** not; **ne . . . personne** no one; **ne . . . plus** no longer; **ne . . . que** only; **ne . . . rien** nothing
**nécessaire** necessary
**neige** *f.* snow
**ni** nor
**noir** black
**nom** *m.* last name
**non** no
**nos** our
**note** *f.* bill
**notre** our
**nous** we, us
**nouveau/elle/el** new
**nuage** *m.* cloud·
**nuageux** cloudy
**nuit** *f.* night
**numéro** *m.* number; **−de téléphone** phone number
**nylon** *m.* nylon

**occuper** occupy; **occupé** busy
**œil, yeux** *m., pl.* eye, eyes
**œuf** *m.* egg
**œuvre** *f.* **(d'art)** work (of art)
**oignon** *m.* onion
**ombre** *f.* shadow
**omelette** *f.* omelet
**orage** *m.* storm
**orange** *m.* orange
**orchestre: à l'−** ground floor
**ordinaire** regular (gas)

**ordonnace** *f.* prescription
**oreille** *f.* ear
**oreiller** *m.* pillow
**ou** or
**où** where
**oublier** forget
**oui** yes
**ouvrir** open; **ouvert** open
**ouvre-boîte** *m.* can opener
**ouvre-bouteille** *m.* bottle opener
**ouvreuse** *f.* usher

**page** *f.* page
**paille** *f.* straw
**pain** *m.* bread
**panne** *f.* breakdown
**panser** dress, bandage
**pantalon** *m.* pants
**papa** Dad
**papeterie** *f.* stationery store
**paquet** *m.* pack
**par** by; **−ici** this way
**parapluie** *m.* umbrella
**parc** *m.* park
**paresseux/se** lazy
**parfait** perfect
**parfum** *m.* perfume
**parking** *m.* parking lot
**parler** speak
**part: de la−de** on behalf of
**partie** *f.* part
**partir** depart, go away
**partenaire** *m., f.* partner
**pas** not; **−du tout** not at all
**passeport** *m.* passport
**passer** pass, go, spend; **−des radios** take some X rays
**pâté** *m.* **(de campagne)** pâté
**pâtisserie** *f.* pastry shop
**payer** pay
**pays** *m.* country
**péage** *m.* (road) toll
**pêche** *f.* peach; fishing
**peigne** *m.* comb
**pellicule** *f.* film
**pendant** during
**penser** think
**pension** *(f.)* **complète** full board
**père** *m.* father
**perdre** lose
**permettre** allow, permit
**permis** *(m.)* **de conduire** driver's license
**personne** *f.* person

89

# VOCABULARY

**petit** little; **—déjeuner** *m.* breakfast;
**—pain** *m.* roll; **—s pois** *m. pl.* peas
**peu** little
**phare** *f.* headlight
**pharmacie** *f.* pharmacy
**pharmacien(ne)** *m., f.* pharmacist
**photographie** *f.* photo, photography
**pièce** *f.* coin
**pied** *m.* foot; **à—** on foot
**pile** *f.* battery
**piquer** string
**piscine** *f.* swimming pool
**place** *f.* square; seat
**plage** *f.* beach
**plaire** please; **ça me plaît** I like it
**plaisir** *m.* pleasure
**plan** *m.* street map
**planche** *(f.)* **à voile** windsurfer
**plaquette** *f.* slab (butter)
**plat** *m.* dish, course: **—cuisiné**
carryout food
**plateau** *(m.)* **de fromage** cheese tray
**plein** full; **faites le—** fill it up (car)
**pleut: il—** it's raining
**pluie** *f.* rain
**plus** more
**plusieurs** several
**plutôt** rather
**pneu** *m.* tire
**poêle** *f.* (frying) pan
**poids lourds** *m. pl.* heavy vehicles
**poignet** *m.* wrist
**pointure** *f.* size (shoe)
**poire** *f.* pear
**poisson** *m.* fish
**poissonnerie** *f.* fish market
**poivre** *m.* pepper
**police** *f.* police; policy; **—d'assurance**
insurance policy
**pommade** *f.* ointment
**pomme** *f.* apple; **—de terre** *f.*
potato
**pompiste** *m., f.* gas station attendant
**pont** *m.* bridge
**porc** *m.* pork
**porcelaine** *f.* porcelain, china
**port** *m.* port, harbor
**porte** *f.* door
**porter** carry, wear
**porte-monnaie** *m.* change purse
**portefeuille** *m.* wallet
**poste** *f.* post (office); **bureau** *(m.)*
**de—** post office
**poste** *m.* extension (tel.)

**potage** *m.* soup
**poudre: en—** granulated
**poulet** *m.* chicken
**pour** for, in order to
**pourboire** *m.* tip
**pourquoi** why
**pousser** push
**pouvoir** be able, can
**préférer** prefer
**premier** first; **—secours** *m.* first aid
**prendre** take
**prénom** *m.* first name
**près de** near
**présenter** introduce, present; **se—**
introduce o.self
**président** *m.* president
**pression** *f.* pressure; draft beer
**prévoir** foresee, forecast
**prix** *m.* price, prize
**professeur** *m., f.* teacher
**produit** *m.* product
**programmeur/se** *m., f.* computer
programmer
**promenade** *f.* walk
**pull(over)** *m.* pullover sweater
**puis** then

**quai** *m.* platform
**quand** when
**quart** *m.* quarter
**que** what, which, that
**quel, quelle** which, that, what
**quelque chose** something, anything
**quelques** a few
**quelqu'un** someone
**qu'est-ce que c'est?** what is it?
**qu'est-ce qu'il y a?** what's the matter?
**qui** who
**quincaillerie** *f.* hardware (store)
**quitter** leave

**raisin** *m.* grape
**râpé** grated
**rapide** *m.* high-speed train
**raser** shave
**rasoir** *m.* razor
**réception** *f.* reception
**recommander** recommend
**réchaud** *m.* stove
**réduction** *f.* reduction
**réduit** reduced
**regarder** look at
**région** *f.* region, district
**règlement** *m.* payment

# VOCABULARY

regretter   regret
rejoindre   join
remède *m.*   remedy
remercier   thank
remplir   fill in
rencontrer   meet; **rencontre** *m.* meeting
rendez-vous *m.*   appointment
renseignements *m. pl.*   information
se renseigner   enquire
repas *m.*   meal
répéter   repeat
se reposer   rest
représentant *m.*   sales representative
réserver   reserve
restaurant *m.*   restaurant
rester   stay
retard: en–   late
retourner   return; **retour** *m.*   return
rez-de-chaussée *m.*   ground floor
rhume *m.*   cold
rivière *f.*   river
riz *m.*   rice
robe *f.*   dress
rognons *m. pl.*   kidneys
rose   pink
rôti   roast
roue *f.*   wheel
rouge   red
route *f.*   road
rue *f.*   street

sac *m.*   (hand)bag; **–de couchage** sleeping bag
saignant   rare
saison *m.*   season
salade *f.*   lettuce, salad
salaire *m.*   salary
salle *f.*   room; **–d'attente**   waiting room; **–de bains**   bathroom; **–de concert**   concert hall
salut   hello
sans   without
saucisse *f.*   sausage
saucisson *m.*   (salami-type) sausage
saumon *m.*   salmon
sauver   save
savoir   know
savon *m.*   soap
séance *m.*   showing, session
secours *m.*   help; **au–!**   help!
secrétaire *m., f.*   secretary
sel *m.*   salt

semaine *f.*   week
sens unique   one-way street
se sentir   feel
service *m.*   service; **–de dépannage** road service
serviette *f.*   napkin; **–de bain**   bath towel; **–hygiénique**   sanitary napkin
seul   alone, only; **seulement**   only
shampooing *m.*   shampoo
si   if
signaler   report
signe *f.*   sign
signer   sign
soif *f.*   thirst; **avoir–**   be thirsty
s'il vous plaît   please
ski *m.*   skiing; **–nautique** waterskiing
slip *m.*   underpants
soie *f.*   silk
soir *m.* **soirée** *f.*   evening
soleil *m.*   sun
son, sa, ses   his, her
sortie *f.*   exit; **–de secours** emergency exit
sortir   go out
soupe *f.*   soup
sous   under
souvent   often
sparadrap *m.*   adhesive bandage
spécialité *f.*   specialty
spectacle *m.*   entertainment, show
stade *m.*   stadium
standardiste *m., f.*   operator
station *(f.)* de métro   subway station
stationnement *m.*   parking
stationner   park
station-service *f.*   service station
sucre *m.*   sugar
super   super (gas)
supermarché *m.*   supermarket
superbe   superb
sur   on
surprise *f.*   surprise
survêtement *m.*   sweatsuit
surveillé   guarded, supervised
syndicat d'initiative *m.*   tourist information office

tabac *m.*   tobacco; **bureau** *(m.)* **de–** tobacco store
table *f.*   table
taille *f.*   size, waist
tailleur *m.*   woman's suit

# VOCABULARY

**tard** late
**tarte** *f.* pie; **—aux pommes** apple pie
**tasse** *f.* cup
**taux** *(m.)* **de change** exchange rate
**taxi** *m.* taxi
**tee-shirt** *m.* T-shirt
**téléphoner** telephone
**température** *f.* temperature
**temps** *m.* time, weather; **à—** on time (train); **à mi—** part-time
**tentation** *f.* temptation
**tente** *f.* tent
**terrain** *(m.)* **de camping** campground
**tête** *f.* head; **—en l'air** scatterbrain
**thé** *m.* tea
**théâtre** *m.* theater
**thon** *m.* tuna
**tiens!** so, well!
**timbre** *m.* stamp; **timbré** stamped
**tir** *(m.)* **à l'arc** archery
**tire-bouchon** *m.* corkscrew
**tirer** pull
**toilettes** *f. pl.* toilets
**tomate** *f.* tomato
**tomber** fall
**ton, ta, tes** your
**tort: en—** in the wrong
**toucher** touch
**toujours** always
**tour** *f.* tower
**tourner** turn
**tournevis** *m.* screwdriver
**tousser** cough
**tout** all; **—droit** straight ahead; **—le monde** everyone; **à—e à l'heure** see you soon; **—près** near, nearby
**toutefois** however
**train** *m.* train
**tranche** *f.* slice
**travail** *m.* work; **travaux** *pl.* road repair
**travailler** work
**traverser** cross
**très** very
**tricostéril** *m.* bandage
**trop (de)** too (much)
**trouver** find; **se—** be found/situated
**truite** *f.* trout

**un, une** a, an
**usine** *f.* factory

**vacances** *f. pl.* vacation

**valise** *f.* suitcase
**varier** vary
**veau** *m.* veal
**vélo** *m.* bicycle
**velours** *m.* velvet
**vendeur/se** *m., f.* salesperson
**vendre** sell
**venir** come
**vent** *m.* wind
**vente** *f.* sale, selling
**ventre** *m.* stomach
**verglas** *m.* ice, icy road
**vérifier** check
**verre** *m.* glass; **—de contact** contact lens
**vert** green
**veste** *f.* jacket
**vêtements** *m. pl.* clothes
**viande** *f.* meat
**vieux/vieille/vieil** old
**ville** *f.* town
**violon** *m.* violin
**vin** *m.* wine
**vinaigre** *m.* vinegar
**virage** *m.* bend
**visite** *f.* visit; **visiter** visit
**vite** quick, quickly
**voici** here is/are
**voie** *f.* track
**voilà** there is/are
**voile** *f.* sail, sailing
**voilier** *m.* sailboat
**voir** see
**voiture** *f.* car
**vol** *m.* theft, flight
**volaille** *f.* poultry
**voler** steal
**voleur** *m.* thief
**volontiers** willingly
**votre, vos** your
**vouloir** wish, want
**vous** you
**voyage** *m.* journey
**voyons** let's see
**vrai** true; **vraiment** really, truly
**vue** *f.* view

**wagon-lit** *m.* sleeping car
**wagon-restaurant** *m.* dining car

**y** there
**yaourt** *m.* yogurt

**zone** *(f.)* **bleue** restricted parking